UNLOCKING THE CODES:

Cleansing Your Bloodline and Breaking Generational Curses

Tara J. Bellamy

Visit the author's website at

www.tarajbellamy.com

Table of Contents

Acknowledgements

❖ To my Lord and Savior Jesus Christ whom I love and adore with my whole heart. You're so good to me. I'm still in awe that you entrusted me with this assignment that is beyond anything I could do on my own. During this journey of healing and restoration, you provided for me, equipped me, strengthened me, and encouraged me to keep moving forward. You sent me out into unknown territories where I had to face giants, obstacles, heartache, and even loss, but I was determined not to let anything or anyone stop me because I knew lives depended on it and healing was needed. You did everything you promised. Thank you for sending me, but the victory belongs to you, Jesus! I love you so much! You're a Good Father.

❖ To my mother, thank you for teaching me about the Lord. I'm forever grateful for your love, your strength, and your patience towards me. You've assisted me in becoming the woman I am today. You're an awesome woman of God, and I love you very much with all my heart.

❖ To my Aunt Regina, thank you for your wisdom, your truths, and revelations regarding the things that I had to see, feel, go through, and heal from these last few years. The revelations you shared helped me to identify my particular areas of struggle, and all of my "whys?" were answered. I thank God for your openness and discernment. I believe when God has something for us to do, He will sometimes appoint certain people in our lives to assist us in completing our ordained assignment. You were one of those amazing people. Thank you for everything.

❖ To all of my pastors and mentors over the years, I'm forever appreciative of your prayers, your wisdom and your guidance. The structure and mentoring that I have received was nothing short of amazing and truly God-ordained. I've been so blessed to have leaders who have made me feel so special and deeply loved. Thank you for your patience, your counsel, and your love.

Dedication

This book is dedicated to people who want change and are seeking and pressing to demolish the repetitive patterns in their lives. May this book be a roadmap and guide to help you through your journey. May the Lord our God give you insight and revelation to overcome every obstacle that is before you! Let it be behind you from this day forth.

YOU WILL UNLOCK THE CODES AND BREAK GENERATIONAL CURSES!

Forward

I have spent many years of my life warning, encouraging, and sharing the gospel with so many. However, I am convinced that many spirit-filled believers live much of their lives oblivious to the demonic realm. Because of the lack of awareness and pursuit of knowledge, the assaults of the enemy are advanced; therefore, illegal territory that does not belong to that kingdom is gained.

The bible records in Hosea 4:6 (KJV), "My people are destroyed for lack of knowledge: because thou hast rejected knowledge, I will also reject thee." This passage gives us insight of how we lose and suffer needlessly because of our unwillingness to become life-long learners and obtainers of knowledge and understanding. There is an old adage that says "What I don't know can't hurt me." I believe this to be false according to scriptural truth. What I don't know can debilitate, hinder, and impede my growth severely. Therefore, knowing our enemy is not just vital, but also of complete necessity in order to win our battles as well as the war.

In Matthew 22:23-29 (ESV), Jesus answered the Sadducees when asked a question concerning the resurrection, "Your mistake is that you don't know the Scriptures, and you don't know the power of God." Our knowledge of scripture has the ability to liberate us. According to St. John 8:32 (KJV), "And ye shall know the truth, and the truth shall make you free." Within the words of these and so many other scriptures exist the power of freedom and liberation from sins power and Satan's lies and deception.

I believe a generation is emerging with fresh eyes, boldness, and fearlessness in speaking and representing the kingdom of God.

Tara Bellamy, in my opinion, is one of those emerging voices. Her openness, honesty, and love for God is placed on display within the pages of this book. She dares to share with her readers her journey through both failures and victories. Often in life, we discover the whys as our lives intersect with the difficulties and challenges we are called to unravel. The problems we are presented with are often the problems we are called to find the answers to. Tara has released in her book the biblical answers to emotional health and healing. I encourage you to read and apply the principles she shares.

Evangelist Regina Espinoza
The Encourager
Founder of R. E. Ministries
Host of W.W.W.O. F. Prayer Call

Introduction

Have you ever known that change was needed in your life, but didn't know where to start? Maybe you feel a tug in your spirit to go in a different direction and do something new, but you don't know where to find the right map to help guide you through the process. Most likely, you have grown up seeing circumstances in the lives of family members and you know that, for whatever reasons, you do not want to go down the same paths.

Now, you're an adult, and you see some of the same patterns being formed in your life that you saw in the lives of other family members. You've seen how they struggle with bitterness and strife when in conflict with others; how they flat out refuse to forgive and harbor unforgiveness…and now you do the same. You watched their broken marriages fall, which resulted in divorce because of adultery or other issues, and now you find yourself going through the same situation. They fell into the sin of fornication, and you witnessed as they struggled to raise children alone. Sometimes there were two to three different fathers not actively involved, and now you're in their same shoes. You saw from afar that their finances were all out of whack as they started sinking into, debt, lack and poverty. The same sicknesses, diseases, and infirmities have plagued your bloodline for years. Homosexuality runs like wild-

1

fire within your bloodline, and now you have these same struggles. Your father was full of pride, arrogance, and deceit. Your mother struggled with lies and anger. Alcoholism and drug use have always been present. Furthermore, frustrations, aggravations, being easily offended, strife and even depression have all been a normal part of your family. Now, fast forward to the present day…You are the spitting image of who they are.

Complicated patterns keep recycling themselves and eventually re-vert themselves right back to YOU. Have you noticed generation after generation of messy dirt that won't wipe clean, of disorder, chaos, and difficulties? You must understand that cycles do not end until someone is bold enough to stop them. Cycles are a series of events that are regularly repeated in the same order. They stay in rotation within the lives of people and are formed when we give the enemy legal access [an opportunity, permission to approach, enter, communicate, and interfere] in our lives. What?! Yes…We've opened ourselves up and given the enemy legal access to enter into our bloodline to form generational curses.

When we sin or place ourselves in atmospheres where we have no business being in, we are allowing the enemy an open portal to slide his way into our lives. Believe it or not, you are partnering in a business deal with Satan. You've signed the papers and sealed the deal without even knowing you were ever seated at the conference room table. And then BOOM!!! A stronghold is formed.

Generational curses are those brought on by our ancestors and passed down from one generation to another. These curses do not come without a cause, a starter, or an originator. Someone in your bloodline opened the door and gave the enemy legal access into his or her life through sin. Lamentations 5:7 (AMP) says, "Our fathers sinned, and are no more; It is we who have carried their sin." Family disorders, dysfunction, and even consequences are repeatedly passed down through the generations by parents through their sin. Now, you find yourself struggling with the same things that your mother or father struggled with even though you tried your hardest not to repeat the cycle.

If any of this that was just mentioned bears a resemblance to your story or if you have worse entanglements, habits, or cycles, then it is possible you have inherited a generational curse. The sin and curse doesn't end in you until someone repents and breaks that curse...AND I want you to know that someone is YOU. You have been chosen to bring the change to your family and your bloodline or else you wouldn't be reading this book. After all, If not YOU, then WHO? The Bible tells us that, "If we [freely] admit that we have sinned and confess our sins, He is faithful and just [true to His own nature and promises], and will forgive our sins and cleanse us continually from all unrighteousness [wrongdoing..]" (1 John 1:9, AMP). Leviticus 26:40-42 also tells us to confess the wickedness of our forefathers. It's up to us to end these cycles now and not let them linger on any longer!

You cannot depend on someone else to ensure your family will live a life full of blessings and deliverance. The truth is no one else is going to fight for "yours" like you can. You can't be lazy, you can't be passive, and you definitely cannot be inconsistent. Do not play any games when it comes to defeating the enemy. He is aggressive, so you have to be just as aggressive with him.

The good news is we can be completely set free from the generational curses that have plagued our families over the years. The bible says WE WILL WIN, and we have victory through our Lord Jesus Christ (1 Corinthians 15:57). We will learn how to leave a godly inheritance and a legacy of blessings instead of curses for

our future generations. We will set future generations up for greatness and leave our children a CLEANSED BLOODLINE. God
wants that for all of us.

❖ *"…I, the Lord your God, am a jealous God, visiting the iniquity
of the fathers upon the children to the third and fourth generations of
those who hate Me, but showing mercy to thousands, to those who love
Me and keep My commandments" (Exodus 20:5-6, ESV).*

Keep on reading! My prayer is that you find the guidance needed
to thoroughly cleanse your bloodline and live a life full of freedom
and generational blessings. In the next few chapters of this book,
we will identify reccurring ungodly patterns and curses that may
be present in your family bloodline throughout the generations…
And then the BREAK will begin.

SECTION 1:

THE REVEAL: FIRST THINGS FIRST

CHAPTER 1

Revelation, Knowledge & Wisdom

❖ *"My people are destroyed for lack of knowledge [of My law, where I reveal My will]. Because you [priestly nation] have rejected knowledge, I also reject you from being My priests. Since you have forgotten the law of your God, I will also forget your children."* *(Hosea 4:6, AMP)*

Revelation is one of the major keys to unlocking the codes. It releases understanding, freedom, liberty, and deliverance in our lives and breaks curses in your bloodline. It's one of the most important truths that we as the body of Christ need today. Often times, revelation is not sought after, but is overlooked as a minor suggestion rather than a major necessity in order to see the things of God clearly. It's crucial to being set free from years of chains, torment, and dysfunction. It gives us details of the big picture and allows light to shine through in dark places.

Without revelation, we will not completely understand God's word or get what we need from it. Think of revelation as being the first few pieces of an extremely difficult puzzle where you start off just matching the colors, images, edges, and corners that are alike in order to build the "big picture". Well, just like puzzles, the missing pieces in our lives are completed and solved as things break in the spirit realm, and the unknown mysteries and misunderstandings are revealed and simplified.

Apokalupsis is the Greek word for revelation and means the unveiling, uncovering, and the revealing of a thing. It is defined as a surprising and previously unknown fact, especially one that is made known in a dramatic way. Revelations will do just that and sometimes will slap you right in the face and make you say, "Why in the world did I not realize that before?" If only we had asked of the Father and sought Him regarding difficult circumstances, revelation would have saved us a lot of grief and turmoil. "He reveals deep and hidden things; He knows what is in the darkness, and the light dwells with Him" (Daniel 2:22, ESV). God will reveal His supernatural insight to you that you did not realize or understand before in His will and timing. Some things only the Father can help us to understand. Ephesians 1:8-9 (AMP) says, "In all wisdom and understanding [with practical insight] He made known to us the mystery of His will according to His good pleasure, which He purposed in Christ." One word from God can change your entire life forever, but it's important for revelation of knowledge to function in your life. Psalms 25:14 (AMP) also says, "The secret [of the wise counsel] of the Lord is for those who fear Him, and He will let them know His covenant and reveal to them] through His word] its [deep, inner] meaning".

So how do we receive revelation? I believe revelation comes from seeking the will of the Father and not our own will when we search Him wholeheartedly and mediate earnestly to hear His voice. The bible says if we seek Him, we will find Him (Deuteronomy 4:29). We want the full understanding and wisdom of His word because we need Him daily in all things and in every area of our lives. We are to be forever learning, gaining knowledge, and going from glory to glory.

You are in a bad place when you feel you know it all. That's a prideful spirit, and pride comes before a great fall according to Proverbs 16:18. Don't ever be so careless that you close your spiritual ears and eyes as mentioned in Matthew 13:11-15. You want to see and really see; hear and really hear, and know that what you are seeing and hearing is from the Lord. We must stay spiritually aware of what's going on around and in us and be ready for whatever may come knowing God has our backs covered.

It's very true that unexpected things happen at the least expectant times and places. You never know when you can expect to hear from the Father because revelation can occur at the most unusual times. So, be sure you are open to receive by seeking His face and His word at all times. At this point, your mind becomes receptive and sensitive to hear from the Lord. Things become clearer, more focused, and you have a lot of "Uh Huh" moments. Your judgment is no longer clouded. The smoke screen is removed, and you're on track and in line with the will of the Father and His purposes for your life. You will be so grateful to God for revealing the truth to you in order for you to move forward in His promises. The Bible says, "A scoffer seeks wisdom and finds none [for his ears are closed to wisdom], but knowledge is easy for the one who understands [because he is willing to learn]" (Proverbs 14:6, AMP). How can you receive revelation from God if you are not living His word? It's free, and all we have to do is apply it to our lives and believe by faith. Let the word do the work. People were completely healed in the bible because of their faith and the trust they had in Jesus' power.

Here is where wisdom comes in, for it means having special unnatural insight. *Sophias* is the Greek word for wisdom. It means full of skill and having knowledge of very diverse matters. Spiritual wisdom comes to those who are receptive to God's word. More and more will be given and supplied unto us as we steady ourselves continuously in Him. Let's ask daily for the Father to provide us with His insight of knowledge and wisdom.

❖ *Daniel 2:19-22 (AMP) says, "Then the secret was revealed to Daniel in a vision of the night, and Daniel blessed the God of heaven. Daniel answered, 'Blessed be the name of God forever and ever, for wisdom and power belong to Him. It is He who changes the times and the seasons; He removes kings and establishes kings. He gives wisdom to the wise and [greater] knowledge to those who have understanding! It is He who reveals the profound and hidden things; He knows what is in the darkness, and the light dwells with Him.'"*

The things of God are sometimes mysterious, but I believe that if you ask for wisdom and if your heart genuinely desires to know Him, He will reveal His purposes to you in simplistic ways that you will understand. We have to dig deep, seek, and search for Him as if He's treasure, (which He is). Psalm 51:6 (AMP) says, "Behold, you desire truth in the innermost being, and in the hidden part [of my heart] you will make me know wisdom."

We all need revelation to take the blinders off of our eyes and see how God sees things. The word of God says, "Call to me and I will answer you, and will tell you great and hidden things that you have not known" (Jeremiah 33:3, ESV). We need revelation, knowledge and wisdom to see the enemy's tactics, tricks, and ploys. The enemy has no new tricks and uses the same scenarios sometimes over and over again in our lives that become cycles and patterns. You've got to be quicker and wiser than him. Don't ever get caught sleeping. The enemy is waiting for us to slip up.

1 Peter 5:8 tells us to stay on guard. Keep your thoughts pure and alert. Being ready at all times so you won't be conformed by the ungodly things of this world, but that your mind will be renewed daily and transformed by the power of God. Then we may prove what is good, acceptable and the perfect will of God. 1 Corinthians 2:16 KJV says, "For who hath known the mind of the Lord, that he may instruct him? But we have the mind of Christ." We must first dig deep and meditate on His word to receive the mind of Christ.

Revelation may not always come in the form that you imagined it would. It may even come from a simple conversation with another person. I will never forget the time I was on the telephone with one of my aunts sharing a horrible situation I was going through at the moment. I had just ended an adulterous relationship that I had been involved in for three months. That's when she revealed to me that my great grandmother, grandmother and others had been involved in the same sin "multiple" times.

At that very moment, I was in utter shock, I was hurt and disappointed. I dropped the phone and began to weep uncontrollably because I knew that it was a cycle that was trying to repeat itself through my family bloodline. It was revelation that was being revealed to me immediately. I believe God allowed that information to be revealed so that I would know exactly how to fight and war the enemy. Truth be told, had my aunt not revealed to me that I was the 4th generation that had faced this issue, my eyes would have only been fixed on my sin, shame and embarrassment when in reality, I was struggling with something that was embedded within my bloodline and it was destined to pop up and occur in my life any day now and possibly even pass down to my children. I had never struggled with the sin of adultery before, or so I thought; but then revelation came knocking. I had been celibate for years and hadn't even gone on a date for quite some time. I was focused on ministry and pleasing the Lord. I questioned God, asking Him, "Where did this all of a sudden come from, and how did I fall so deep and so fast?" He brought back to my memory years prior when I had dated married, but separated men going through divorces. I thought it was okay since they had been separated for quite some time, didn't have any contact with their spouses, and lived in a different city, it was okay. Ladies and gentlemen, they are STILL MARRIED and you are committing adultery. Thank God for His grace, mercy, and revelation knowledge that shows us our wrongs even when we think it's all good; that mercy and grace that keeps and protects us even in our mess. Revelation will sometimes chase you down, and God will say, "Enough is enough; it's time she knows the truth and sees her sins clearly." Cycles, patterns, and curses are sometimes in us and we don't even know it. We cannot even detect them. I'll share more of my struggle with adultery in a later chapter. I give all praise to God for revealing His truths to me!

❖ *"If you continue to accept and obey my teaching, you are really my followers. You will know the truth, and the truth will make you free." (John 8:31-32, ERV).*

The devil is a liar and will taunt you and make you think only you are going through your struggles. I firmly believe that is why it is important to ask your parents, aunts, uncles, whoever, "How did this pattern start?" The issue many have is they don't know how to connect the dots to find the beginning of the problem. They are rootless and don't know where they came from.

Additionally, it is especially important to ask your spouse questions about his or her family as well. Some problems need to be revealed, especially if the same issues keep recycling in the family with the same horrible end results. You MUST know what you are up against so that you know how to spiritually handle, break and destroy these strongholds in your life.

❖ *"Where there is no revelation, the people perish; but he that keepth the law, happy is he." (Proverbs 29:18, KJV).*

God wants to reveal to us the dark places in our lives so that we can receive healing and deliverance. Those secret things that are hard to understand, guess what, they don't have to stay secret and hard to understand. We can receive the codes to unlock God's blessings for our lives. Our God is a revealer of secretes. He gives us His wisdom freely so we can become wiser and go from glory to glory to glory. He wants us to learn His ways and etch his word on our hearts so that we will always remember it, especially in time of need and trouble.

❖ *Deuteronomy 29:29 (ESV) says, "The secret things belong to the Lord our God, but the things that are revealed belong to us and to our children forever, that we may do all the words of this law."*

Once we receive revelation regarding the things that concern us, our lives will become clearer and more visible to our spiritual minds and eyes. We are no longer behind the darkened curtain that once blocked us from seeing and getting to our Savior (our audience of 1), and no longer will we be left in the darkness. When we are not playing in sin, but truly living for our Savior, our minds become receptive to hear from God. One of our number one goals should be to know more about the things of God and what He wants for our lives. The more knowledge we receive, the wiser we become. We are able to put His word to work more effectively in our lives because we are in alignment with Him and the plan He has for us. As we become more intimate with our Savior and are able to know what God's plan is for us, then we are effectively able to move and operate daily in the things of God. We will know and have the heart of God, which is truly a gift from Him.

"But if they do not listen, they perish by the sword and die without knowledge" (Job 36:12, ESV). Surely, you do not want to be destroyed and die a spiritual death just because you are too lazy and/or foolish to fight for change in your life and in the lives of others in your family. Get what you need to overcome. Revelation, Knowledge, and Wisdom combined are a force to be reckoned with. This three-stranded cord produces sincere supernatural guidance and counsel that you can't receive from anywhere or anyone else but our Heavenly Father. Your frequencies and connectors MUST align with His purposes and destination, meaning having an attitude of "not my will, but yours, Father be done in my life". Learning how to move in perfect harmony with Him will take you to a higher level of understanding.

❖ *Ephesians 1:17 (ESV) tells us that the God of our Lord Jesus Christ, the Father of glory, may give unto you the spirit of wisdom and revelation in the knowledge of him, having the eyes of your hearts enlightened, that you may know what is the hope to which he has called you, what are the riches of his glorious inheritance in the saints, and what is the immeasurable greatness of his power toward us who believe, according to the working of His great might…"*

Declaration Prayer

Father God, my Lord and Savior, I pray and ask for the knowledge of insight, wisdom, guidance, and revelation that only You can give me. I pray that any unknown secrets and mysteries will be revealed in my life and will enable me to break free from the sins that once held me bound. Lord, assist, guide, and direct me in reaching the divine purpose that you have destined for my life that will ultimately catapult me into a life of cleansing, deliverance, and freedom in Christ Jesus. AMEN.

So, now that we know we first need revelation, let the revealing begin.

Generational Bloodline Curses

Generational curses are curses that have been brought on by our ancestors and passed down from one generation to another. As mentioned earlier, Curses do not come without a cause, a start, and an originator. Someone in your bloodline and family history opened the door and gave the enemy legal access into their life through sin. Lamentations 5:7 (AMP) says, "Our fathers sinned, and are no more; it is we who have carried their sin." The devil just can't pop in anytime he wants; he has to have access. When we are out of place, disconnected, or disobedient, we are giving him that access into our lives. "Neither give place to the devil" (Ephesians 4:27, KJV). Don't give the enemy an opportunity to lead you to sin.

Family disorders, dysfunction, and even consequences are repeatedly passed down through the generations by parents through their sin. Struggles keep cycling through from great grandmother, to grandmother, to mother, and now you are struggling with the same exact issues, even though you tried your hardest not to repeat the cycle. Bishop TD Jakes once said, "Someday or another, you will have to deal with your daddy's devil."

As mentioned earlier in this book, cycles are a series of events that are regularly repeated in the same order. They stay on rotation in the lives of people and families and are formed when we give the enemy legal access [opportunity, permission to approach, enter, communicate, and interfere] to enter into our bloodline to form generational curses. The enemy has to have an entry point of contact, and that contact is sin. When we sin, we open a portal or door for the enemy to enter into our lives legally and remain until we repent, rebuke, renounce, and live opposite of the sin.

Demons need our bodies in order to operate and wreak havoc on this earth. They are bad spirits that need us in order to function and act up. They wait on you to take the second look at that woman and lust after her. They wait for you to flirt with that man knowing he is married. They tempt and wait for you to take that sip and light that pipe up. Demons teeter back and forth and wait for us to make a bad decision or choice. Then, they come in to convince us to stay in that bad place of sin. Therefore, we are not to entertain those thoughts, but to cast down every imagination that does not line up with the word of God.

We cannot give the enemy legal reign to control our thoughts that end up controlling our actions. When we confess our sins, God forgives. If the sin remains, the enemy has a ball trying to destroy our lives, thereby causing delay and holding us back from fulfilling God's promises for our lives. When we sin or enter ourselves in situations and covenants we are not supposed to be in or apart of, we are allowing the enemy an open portal to slide his way into our lives. You are partnering in a business deal with Satan. The contract was placed in front of you. You have signed on the dotted line and sealed the deal without even realizing you were ever at the conference table, and now strongholds are formed.

In Deuteronomy 30, God gives us two choices to choose life or death. One choice will bring a blessing, and the other will bring a curse. So choose life, and you and your children will live and not die a spiritual death. We have to love the Lord and obey Him so that sin and iniquities will not come in and thrive for generations and generations. God is life to us and the air we breathe. We put our future, hopes, and dreams in His hands, but the enemy wants nothing more than to kill and destroy our legacy. He wants to taint our bloodline and mix in multiple toxins so we can't see the truth or figure out how to get healed and delivered from the sickness. But God promised long life to us and our children through His word. We can be free from those curses and cycles.

A curse has a legal right to operate and act up in the way it does over and over again without being charged or arrested by the court of law. It's like it has free reign to do what it wants. That is, until we stand up against the enemy. When we know our rights, when we know the law, when we know our authority and what we are entitled to, we can take down the strongholds in our lives and destroy them forever.

There are spiritual laws that are in operation, and the devil is the prosecutor of the brethren. That's why Jesus needs to be your attorney in the courtroom working and fighting on your behalf. Call Him up. Better yet, stop by unannounced and knock on His door, He will work on your behalf pro bono. Revelation 3:20 says that Jesus stands at the door and waits for us to see if we are willing to allow Him direct permission to come into our lives. Bring your problems to the courts of heaven where our God who is the ultimate judge, defender, healer, waymaker, and who helps us and fights on our behalf. We cannot let the devil utilize legalities that can stop us from entering into our destiny. We have authority to release God's true blessings and destiny over our lives.

We've read in God's word that Jesus has already paid the price for generational curses. Jesus was made a curse so that we would become free. "Christ hath redeemed us from the curse of the law, being made a curse for us: for it is written, cursed is everyone that hangeth on a tree" (Galatians 3:13, KJV).

Iniquities are sins that are guilty and worthy of punishment. A curse is that punishment. Psalms 51:5 says, "Behold, I was brought forth in iniquity and in sin my mother conceived me." A reasonable question to ask is: Why are we dealing with these things in our lives? In John 9, Jesus' followers asked him why was the man born blind? Was it because of his parents' sin or his own? Let's remember to pray for revelation.

Let's take a look at a couple people in the bible who had some generational issues going on in their families.

Abraham's bloodline had quite a few liars in it. Everyone seemed to have had a lying spirit.

- ♣ Abraham lied about Sarah being his wife and said she was his sister (Gen. 20).

- ♣ Abraham's son Isaac lied about his wife (Gen 26).

- ♣ Isaac's son is found lying and deceived his father so that he couwld get the birthright (Genesis 27). Lies and deception continued on throughout the family.

King David's bloodline was filled with lust, adultery, and incest.

- ♣ David's great, great grandmother was a prostitute (Joshua 2).

- ♣ David had an affair with a married woman named Bathsheba and then had her husband Uriah killed on the frontlines so that he could have her to himself (2 Samuel 11).

- ♣ David's son Amnon raped his sister Tamar (2 Samuel 13).

♣ David's son, Solomon, had over 1,000 wives and concubines (1 Kings 11).

We see lust, incest and perversion running rapid David's bloodline.

We are weak from sins that have been passed down to us. Our flesh is uncontrollably weak; therefore, we are unable to overcome these strongholds. Generational curses get bigger and stronger as the generations go on, and they become giants until you and come along and defeat every single last one of them in your life. These demonic strongholds and battles that are in place in our lives are because we are wrestling and fighting with what our forefathers never defeated; therefore, it's up to us to win the war.

When we are able to recognize and change the patterns in our families, we are on the right track, a track and a path that will lead us right into victory through Jesus Christ. One of the reasons why the things you witnessed and observed never sat well with you growing up was because you were the one ordained to break it. Be that change that you want to see.

The good thing about patterns is they can be traced. We can connect the dots right back to the originator. A family pattern that keeps continuing has never ending results. It's a circle that keeps recycling over and over again. We have to get to the core of the problem and where it all started. If we find the cause, we can eliminate it at its roots. What is the bad fruit that is being produced and grown in your life? What's the root of it?

Jesus' Bloodline / Knowing who you are in Christ

I'll tell you something you probably did not know. Even people with toxic blood, awful reputations, and who have made bad decisions can be purged, cleansed, and set free. We see this happen in the Bible with Rahab, Tamar, and Bathsheba, and they all had a part in the royal bloodline of Jesus. God honors our efforts to want better as we do better and make the necessary changes in our lives. Let us thank God for His Cleansing power! The Lord speaks about cleansing our dirty bloodlines in Joel 3:21 (MSG). "The sins I haven't already forgiven, I'll forgive."

Believe it or not, we all have the good stuff running through our veins. It's that blood that cannot be tainted once it's been touched by the glory of Jesus. It's the blood that washes us whiter than snow. It brings sanctification, healing and deliverance. It restores family situations and brings our bodies back to their originally intended functionalities. We are forgiven and redeemed through His blood and never forsaken. We have overcome Satan and his plots and ploys. In the song, "The blood will never lose its power", the lyrics say, "It gives us strength from day to day, and it will never lose its power." It continues on and on for generations to come. The cleaning solution is free of charge, we just have to tap in and receive the offering. Allow the Father to wash and cleanse you from all filth and unrighteousness. He will do it. He has ransomed us and set us free. We do not have to stay in darkness and off course, but we are guided by Jesus who keeps us on the godly path of righteousness.

If we knew and recognized our true identity in Christ, we would never stand for just anything entering us that is not of God. If we had the faith to believe who our Daddy really is, we wouldn't fear, we wouldn't have doubts, and we would tell Him everything that is trying to attack us knowing that our Father will fight on our behalf and will always win. We can always depend on this covering just because of whom we are related to and what runs through our bloodline.

Like Abraham was chosen to be the father of many nations [numerous future generations], we have to be determined to declare that our future generations will be blessed and that they will be set free and delivered. We are exactly who our Father says we are, and we can do exactly what He says we can do in any circumstance.

❖ *"And if you are Christ's, then you are Abraham's seed, and heirs according to the promise." (Galatians 3:29 ESV)*

We are royalty, and we have royal DNA running through our veins. We are to reign in life as such kings and queens [children of the most high God]. The bible says we are a chosen generation, a royal priesthood, a holy nation, a peculiar people [God's special possession], that you may declare the praises of Him who called you out of darkness into His wonderful light. We have to get our original blood circulating in us so much, the devil won't know what is going on and will have to leave. Oil and vinegar cannot mix. Light and darkness cannot come into agreement. Where there is light, darkness is vanquished. As mentioned earlier, divine revelation comes from the Lord to show us the light and the way out of our problems and situations. We have to know our history and our background in order to find out what happened in our bloodline.

Your DNA has a really good memory. It remembers every area of struggle, sickness, disease, sexual sins, problems, and so forth that has ever happened in our lives. That's how it is able to reciprocate and trickle down the line. It also remembers the good lines, the health, the prosperity, the good habits, the discipline, the right thinking, and the financial prayers sown.

Many problems are caused because of what's in our bloodline and the answers to all of our problems have been freely given to us through the blood of Jesus Christ. It's a great exchange. We give

Him our problems, and He gives us freedom from whatever was holding us back in guilt and pain. Nothing but the blood of Jesus can fix us like that!

After recognizing and pinpointing these areas, we will walk through how to legally break off everything in our bloodlines that does not line up with God. In the next chapters, let's identify common curses that are plaguing family bloodlines. I pray that God will specifically give you revelation to identify specific curses that are in your bloodline.

IDENTIFYING REPETITIVE CURSES AND CYCLES

CHAPTER 2

Generational Bondage

❖ *"That creation would be set free from decay and would share in the glorious freedom of His children." (Romans 8:21, CEV)*

Did you know that people are enslaved by their thinking? Bondage is defined as the state of being a slave. People who are in bondage believe they have restricted freedom. They have no ambition; no vision and no direction for promotion and prosperity. They sometimes don't believe they can ever do better or be better in life. At this point, their minds are closed to hearing from God to receive freedom, instruction and deliverance in certain areas of their lives.

They keep roaming around in circles living in the same area, and being around the same, no good, stinking thinking people. They are negative and take time to learn more or grow further in Christ. Anything that takes real effort, they aren't willing to do, and they make excuses not to do it. They may have something in them that wants to change, but it's like their minds are paralyzed from making a move forward and stepping out of the box. Spirits of laziness and unproductiveness has a root of bondage. There's no progression or growth.

Spiritual bondage will also have you deep in sin. Evil has its schemes and ways to enslave your mind. He (the devil) is evil "d-evil." He has a way of taking over people's lives and making it hard for them to get away from the negative norm that he developed for them to stay stuck in. When in bondage, it's like having a zombie like mentality.

> ❖ *"They promised freedom to everyone. But they are merely slaves of filthy living, because people are slaves of whatever controls them." (2 Peter 2:19, CEV)*

What has control over you? Is it your thoughts? Could it be your circumstances, such as finances or relationships? Have you allowed them to become your master and have been subjected to them under bondage? When evil spirits are allowed in, they come and they plan to stay for as long as they are allowed. They want to dig deeper and penetrate harder. Their plan is to leave as much damage to people's lives as possible. They bring with them sin and confusion, so that you can't understand how to find a way out. Bondage will paralyze you and stop you from accomplishing things God assigned you to do. He's given you courage and boldness to succeed in every area of your life, but you are too afraid to step out and do it.

> ❖ *"Jesus said, the truth is, everyone who sins is a slave to sin. A slave does not stay with a family forever. But a son belongs to the family forever. So if the son makes you free, you are really free." (John 8:34-36, ERV)*

Bondage wants you to stay still, scared, remain in sin and other dysfunctions and not be promoted. But God's perfect love casts out fear.

> ❖ *"The Spirit that we receive is not a spirit that makes us slaves again and causes us to fear. The Spirit that we have makes us God's chosen children. And with that Spirit we cry out, Abba, Father. And the Spirit himself speaks to our spirits and makes us sure that we are*

God's children. If we are God's children, we will get the blessings God has for his people. He will give us all that he has given Christ..." *(Romans 8:15-17, ERV)*

When you are trying to make a change in your life and break some things off, you cannot remain in your old way of thinking. You cannot operate in the same mode. If the spirit of bondage is one of your struggles, you may have to change your focus and your environment completely. By stepping out of an arena that you aren't comfortable with shows effort, and God honors our efforts when they're in His will.

- ❖ *"And everyone who has left houses or brothers or sisters or father or mother or wife or children or fields for my sake will receive a hundred times as much and will inherit eternal life." (Matthew 19:29, NLT)*

- ❖ *"For freedom Christ has set us free; stand firm therefore, and do not submit again to a yoke of slavery." (Galatians 5:1, ESV)*

- ❖ *"I am the Lord your God, who brought you out of the land of Egypt, out of the house of slavery." (Exodus 20:2, ESV)*

- ❖ *"But it is because the Lord loves you and is keeping the oath that He swore to your fathers, that the Lord has brought you out with a mighty hand and redeemed you from the house of slavery, from the hand of Pharaoh King of Egypt." (Deuteronomy 7:8, ESV)*

- ❖ *"Jesus became like these people and died so that he could free them. They were like slaves all their lives because of their fear of death." (Hebrews 2:15, ERV)*

- ❖ *"Now, the Lord is the Spirit, and where the Spirit of the Lord is, there is freedom." (2 Corinthians 3:17, ERV)*

- ❖ *"Do not be conformed to this world, but be transformed by the re-*

newal of your mind, that by testing you may discern what is the will of God, what is good and acceptable and perfect." (Romans 12:2, ESV)

Declaration Prayer

Father, I repent for myself and those in my bloodline that have been entangled in any form of bondage. Search me, oh God, and break any agreements of bondage in my bloodline. I take the sword of the spirit that cuts me loose and frees me from slavery mindsets. Thank you for releasing me from the yoke of chains and stagnation. I receive my deliverance and leave no place for bondage in my mind or spirit. I am free from it, and who the Son sets free is free indeed. I see clearer and possess the mind of Christ Jesus. The chains of negativity are gone in my life because Christ has redeemed me. Freedom belongs to me. Thank you for the breakthrough in my life. I am no longer bound by the enemy in Jesus' Name.

CHAPTER 3

Generational Poverty & Lack

❖ *"And my God will meet all your needs according to His glorious riches in Christ Jesus." (Philippians 4:19, KJV)*

B
ondage plays a major part in generational curses of poverty and lack. If people don't believe they can live an abundant life, then they will never get out of the pit of less than and not enough. Their minds are not renewed or opened to receive basic instruction and principles on poverty release. The spirit of poverty promotes not having enough, living in hardship, shortage, lack, and insufficiency. Lack and poverty mindsets begin because of a person's lack of trust in God.

You don't believe you can do better, so you don't spiritually act on the fact that it is possible. You may read the scriptures, but do not have enough faith to actually stand on the word of God until you see the change. You give up too quickly; almost instantly. You have to overcome unbelief and doubting in God. It is crucial to growing in Christ in any area of your life, not just in your finances. If you consider Him your Lord and Savior, then you should believe that He can save you out of whatever spirit or circumstance that is tripping you up. Right?

Well, that's the way it's supposed to work, but we default on our own prosperity by not applying God's word to work in our lives and by not speaking and praying the scriptures over ourselves and our family. The end result is you remain in the bondage of poverty, and your children end up going through the same stress and issues.

Your mom lived in the housing projects, her mom lived there, and so do you. You don't even see that there is an entirely different world outside the gates of that housing community. You've never explored or even attempted to make a move or do better because you are too comfortable. I believe that government help is a great form of assistance that bridges a need gap, but when it is abused and used beyond a reasonable timeframe, it becomes a crutch and enables that mindset to continue. Just as people can have a mindset of lack, they can renew their minds to a mindset of wealth and riches. Change is a part of growth and development. We should not be in the same space spiritually as we were a year ago. Cindy Trimm challenges you to be better than you were three months ago.

Unless it brings glory to God such as consistent prayer, reading, praise, worship, and so forth, get out of the repeated cycles. Leave an example for your children to want more of the things of God. It's important to train your children on financial wisdom, growth, and prosperity. They must have a trained mind to know that if there is a need; God will supply it because His word says He will.

❖ *"Ask and it will be given to you; seek, and you will find; knock and it will be opened to you." (Matthew 7:7, ESV)*

Locusts

The color green signifies growth, prosperity, and healing. Locusts are insects that are attracted to anything that looks good, green, whole, and healthy in our lives. Locust swarm and eat everything that is flourishing physically and spiritually. They breed at rapid rates and have the potential to wreak havoc in our lives. Even when things aren't looking so good, locust will still come and attempt to get the very last bit of whatever is left in us.

You may say "Every time I get a little extra money, something always comes up". These spirits come to suck you dry. They don't want to see you blessed and have every intention to keep you low and empty. But there is a promise of restoration in Joel 2:25 (KJV), "The Lord says, 'And I will restore to you the years that the locusts hath eaten, the cankerworm, and the caterpillar, and the palmerworm, my great army which I sent among you." The Lord will rebuke whatever is devouring your blessings. Whatever the enemy has stolen, it can be return back to you. It's called recompense; meaning to make amends to someone for loss or harm suffered; to compensate.

You can and will stop the enemy in his tracks and reverse and defeat the repeated cycles of poverty within your family. Life will be restored back unto you and stolen blessings will be repaid.

Tithes and Offerings

If you have never tithed before or have never really been a consistent tither, tithing can be a challenge to your faith, but how will you know if you don't try? God said, "Test me". I remember when my adult children were young and started receiving $1 here or $5 there, I would teach them the principle of tithing. When they became older and began working jobs as teens, I never had to remind them about tithing. They may have had a few "missed payments" but as a parent, I would gently make sure they got back on track and they continued. By me starting when they were young, the seed of sowing and reaping was planted on the inside of them.

Some may say they can't afford to tithe, but the reality is, they can't afford NOT to tithe. When you sacrifice from your hands, God brings it right back to you and then some. We are to give freely and not grudgingly. Not holding things for selfish gain, but wise in our affairs and the word of God says to "Give, and it will be given to you..." (Luke 6:38, NKJV).

❖ *"..Bring the entire ten percent into the storehouse, so there will be food in my house. Then I will open the windows of heaven and flood you with blessing after blessing." (Malachi 3:10, CEV)*

Who's Your Source?

I believe people panic and attempt to bring wealth on their own by relying on their jobs and other man-made finance areas to survive in life. But when you know that God is your provider and that your ONLY source is HIM, then you are able live free from fear of lack and poverty. Your position at work is not your source. The only way to secure any area in your life is through Him. He is the one who causes us to get wealth.

When you are in continual debt and lack, you most likely have not been a good steward over the things that you have; therefore, it's difficult for you to manage your money properly and utilize the financial principles in God's word. Robbing Peter to pay Paul, being in debt, and owing others money are not in God's will. We are to be lenders and not borrowers. Romans 13:8 says that you should owe nothing to anyone, except that you will always owe love to each other. Yet, unwise people keep adding more and more debt to credit cards. They continuously take out payday loans and buy furniture at rent to own centers. The poverty mindset has never owned anything of its own, only used credit to make purchases.

Owning a home or paying cash for a vehicle has never crossed their minds. Poverty and lack mindsets live in the "right now" and they spend what little money they do have instantly.

❖ *"The wise have wealth and luxury, but fools spend whatever they get."* (Proverbs 21:20, NLT)

What if you have a spending problem? These are those who waste their money on frivolous things that they really do not need. No food in the house for the kids, but are at the nail salon every single week. Some are more concerned with material wealth of shoes, clothes and jewelry, yet their homes are a mess; they may not even have a kitchen table and have mattresses on the floor. Not because they couldn't actually purchase these things, but because their priorities are all out of order and going in so many different directions.

Instead of looking up and staying focused on Him, they're looking every which a way. They have never been taught by anyone on how to get and maintain money. Simple rules that would normally be considered common sense to most are bizarre to them. When you are a good steward over your money, you understand that it is unwise to make purchases or charges with high interest rates. You will never pay them off, but the poverty mentality says, "I want it, and I want it now no matter what. I will find a way to pay it later."

❖ *"The rich rules over the poor, and the borrower is the slave to the lender."* (Proverbs 22:7, ESV)

How's your stewardship? We are to show honor in the things we have been blessed with; not only with our money, but also in our ministries, marriages, jobs, homes, and other areas. Can God trust you to take care of those things? He's given us great responsibility.

Are we just doing the minimum and only maintaining, or do you go above and beyond to show God "Yes" this is yours, and I will honor you by taking extra care of this thing you have placed me charge over…this thing you've given me dominion over. "To whom much is given, much is expected. "(Luke 12:48, KJV).

Financial curses are planted in the bloodline to keep people from prospering. Generations are continuously in debt, subjected to bill collectors and payment arrangements each and every month, and are always looking for free handouts. I mean we all like free stuff, but what are your motives behind how you go about getting the free stuff? Do you lie, cheat and steal to get it? Do you manipulate people by wanting them to feel sorry for you and your situation? That's manipulation! Putting pressure on other people as if you are their responsibility; that's manipulation! They wonder why the little that they have is stolen right out their hands. They hold what they have and do not share or pay their tithes and offerings. They see no point or benefit in it. This mindset never gets ahead, and blessings are minimum and limited due to their own doing and/or "not doing".

❖ *"In daylight you will have to feel your way like a blind man. You will fail in everything you do. Again and again people will hurt you and steal from you and there will be no one to save you." (Deuteronomy 28:29, ERV)*

❖ *"The blessing of the Lord makes a person rich, and he adds no sorrow with it." (Proverbs 10:22, ESV)*

The bible says that He would rebuke the devour for our name sake (Malachi 3:11, KJV). The paycheck to paycheck living can be reversed and having more than enough can be applied to your life.

Wealth Blessings

I believe that God wants us to be blessed to be a blessing. It is not God's will for us to feel less than or live in the less than. We are the head and not the tail. That means we have power, and that power comes with entitlement. God wants the best for you in your finances, but you have to trust that He will provide for you and your family. He knows what we need before we even say a word, so why worry? Why continue to struggle with lack when He's got our best interest at heart? Where's your faith?

God's word isn't there just for nothing. It shows us exactly who our God is and what He can do in our lives. "I AM THAT I AM" means "He Is EVERYTHING". There's nothing missing in Him that needs to be filled. He is our everything, and if we are made in His image, that means we do not lack anything either. Seek God in every financial area. Seek Him before every purchase and financial decision. Stand no other way but completely on His promises, He is bigger than what you see in the natural.

Your view of the impossible is God's reality that can change any situation just like that. God's will shall be done just as it is in heaven, but you have to believe. Pray for God to help your unbelief! Your belief will get stronger and stronger until it is unshakeable. Your faith will activate supernatural debt release over your life. All demonic spirits that are behind the poverty, lack, and debt in your life will be demolished and erased through the help of our Lord and Savior.

❖ *"For the Lord God will help me; therefore shall I not be confounded: therefore have I set my face like a flint, and I know that I shall not be ashamed." (Isaiah 50:7, KJV)*

He's here to help and wants to help. The cycled bondage will have no other choice but to go when you begin to declare what God's word says about your situation. You have authority over Satan. Open your eyes to recognize the areas you and your family struggle in. Once revealed you will be able to go after that thing with strategy (God's word). God will give you discipline and knowledge to overcome and win in your area of struggle. Stand strong and do not be shaken by what you see. It will be worth the fight in the end. You should want to leave your children and your children's children financial blessings and not poverty curses. Transfer wealth and riches to them. Decree and declare it over your bloodline.

❖ *"Thou shalt also decree a thing, and it shall be established unto thee: and the light shall shine upon thy ways." (Job 22:28, KJV)*

❖ *"For verily I say unto you, that whosoever shall say unto this mountain, be thou removed, and be thou cast into the sea; and shall not doubt in his heart, but shall not doubt in his heart, but shall believe that those things which he saith shall come to pass; he shall have whatsoever he saith." (Mark 11:23, KJV)*

❖ *"Good people leave an inheritance to their grandchildren, but the sinner's wealth passes to the godly." (Proverbs 13:22, NLT)*

❖ *"Then the Lord your God will bless you, as he promised. And you will have enough money to make loans to many nations. But you will not need to borrow from anyone. You will rule over many nations. But none of these nations will rule over you." (Deuteronomy 15:6 ERV)*

❖ *"But blessed are those who trust in the Lord and have made the Lord their hope and confidence. They are like trees planted along a riverbank, with roots that reach deep into the water. Such trees are not bothered by the heat or worried by long months of drought. Their* leaves stay green, and they never stop producing fruit." (Jeremiah 17:7-8, NLT)

❖ "God is the one who gives seed to those who plant, and he gives bread for food. And God will give you spiritual seed and make that seed grow. He will produce a great harvest from your goodness. God will make you rich in every way so that you can always give freely. And your giving through us will make people give thanks to God." (2 Corinthians 9:10, ERV)

❖ "Give, and you will receive. Your gift will return to you in full-pressed down, shaken together to make room for more, running over, and poured into your lap. The amount you give will determine the amount you get back." (Luke 6:38, NLT)

❖ "Honor the Lord with your wealth and with the best part of everything you produce. Then he will fill your barns with grain, and your vats will overflow with good wine." (Proverbs 3:9-10, NLT)

❖ "And this same God who takes care of me will supply all your needs from his glorious riches, which have been given to us in Christ Jesus." (Philippians 4:19, NLT)

❖ "And God will generously provide all you need. Then you will always have everything you need and plenty left over to share with others." (2 Corinthians 9:8, NLT)

Declaration Prayer

Forgive me, Father, for times when myself or others in my family have been unwise with our money. Bring structure and order back in this area of my life. Thank you, Jehovah Jireh, for being my source and providing everything I need. Lord, you have left me a wealth inheritance that I receive right now. I decree financial freedom, financial wisdom, and financial discernment within my life and my bloodline. I will receive financial blessings of wealth and riches as I honor you and give of my tithes and offerings. I will never think twice or be double-minded about sharing with others or giving.

My faith and trust in you will expound beyond what my eyes can see, and because I tithe, doors will be opened unto me and those connected to me. I speak generational wealth in all areas of my life, and I receive strategies to defeat that which attempts to devour my finances. Debt release is Mine! Freedom is Mine! Money Cometh to Me! Lord, grow my wealth! Exceed my expectations! I command financial connections and blessings to find me and attach to me. My money will fall in line with God's word and do exactly what God intended it to do for me because I am His child. I am a good steward over it. My money will work for me in the Name of Jesus!

CHAPTER 4

Generational Anger and Rebellion

❖ *"Refrain from anger, and forsake wrath! Fret not yourself; it tends only to evil. For evildoers shall be cut off, but those who wait for the Lord shall inherit the land." (Psalm 37:8-9, ESV)*

Anger and rage grips onto lives and causes people to have unpredictable and misguided judgment calls that end up changing their lives in one quick second; all because they did not take the time to calm down and not let their anger get the best of them.

Anger is a strong feeling or emotion of annoyance, displeasure or hostility. It makes people feel that they have been wronged or hurt by someone. Actually, the foundation of anger is hurt and pain. At some point, there was a level of hurt that occurred where they felt like they had been done wrong, betrayed, unloved, or even misguided. Spirits of anger cause people to be offended easily, in conflict, and have aggression towards others. Frustrations will taunt you and spirits of aggravation will bring thoughts of anxiety, fear, depression and weariness. If these thoughts and feelings are not cast down and defeated, they will pass down to future generations.

❖ *"Do not take heart all the things that people say, lest you hear your servant cursing you. Your heart knows that many times yourself have cursed others." (Ecclesiastes 7:21-22, ESV)*

Anger can also erupt when unexpected outcomes occur. That's why it's important to keep your cool when things happen. The bible says, "Be angry and do not sin; do not let the sun go down on your anger and give no opportunity to the devil." (Ephesians 4:26, ESV).

Attachments of anger include unforgiveness, rejection, failure, strife, envy, and revenge; so not only do we have to deal with and harbor all of these other illnesses, we now struggle to overcome them as well. When dealing with multiple emotional issues, we can do some crazy things. Saul was jealous, bitter, fearful, and angry with David and tried to have him killed in 1 Samuel 19:10. Sometimes, we can be upset with people, and they have no idea what they even did to upset us in the first place. Some are easily offended and think everyone is out to get them. Others refuse to let go and make peace. And don't believe for one second that just because it's been years since you've seen that person and you haven't thought about them, your anger is gone. It has actually been left undealt with for all those years. Anger will lay dormant and wait for the right time to pop back up. Angry people are like a ticking time bomb allowing things to build instead of putting them completely away.

❖ *"But now you also, put them all aside: anger, wrath, malice, slander, and abusive speech from your mouth." (Colossians 3:8, NASB)*

Not knowing how to control your anger can get you into serious trouble. One rebellious decision can cost you your ministry, your marriage, your job, or much worst. It can cause you to make hasty decisions that you later regret. Poor choices that we make affect our future generations and those currently connected to us. Don't pass anger and rebellion down. Get to the root of problem and stop it quickly. Angry kids grow up to be angry adults trying to deal with problems that were just covered up by messy layers. These layers need to be revealed so that the healing process can begin. Don't say things out of anger by being caught up in the moment. Hold your tongue not only in speech, but also in spirit and most importantly, guard your heart.

So, how do you respond to adversity? Peace must be your stance and position. You can't let anger control who you really are. Overpower it by maintaining your peace and keeping the word of God in your heart. There are a lot of scriptures in the bible that deal with anger. Maybe because it is a very common stronghold that the enemy uses to keep us bound.

You have to remember to walk and remain in the love of God. Without walking in love, you'll find yourself engaging in sinful acts of rage and regret. It's important to find the root of a thing and what makes you tick, so that you can confront it and deal with the thing according to the word of God.

❖ *"What causes quarrels and what causes fights among you? Is it not this, that your passions are at war within you? You desire and do not have, so you murder. You covet and cannot obtain, so you fight and quarrel. You do not have, because you do not ask." (James 4:1-2, ESV)*

❖ *"Know this, my beloved brothers: let every person be quick to hear, slow to speak, slow to anger, for the anger of man does not produce the righteousness of God." (James 1:19-20, ESV)*

❖ *"Make no friendship with a man given to anger, nor go with a wrathful man, lest you learn his ways and entangle yourself in a snare." (Proverbs 22:24-25, ESV)*

❖ *"A fool gives full vent to his spirit, but a wise man quietly holds it back." (Proverbs 29:11, ESV)*

❖ *"Good sense makes one slow to anger, and it is his glory to overlook an offense." (Proverbs 19:11, ESV)*

❖ *"A soft answer turns away wrath, but a harsh word stirs up anger." (Proverbs 15:1, ESV)*

❖ *"A hot-tempered man stirs up strife, but he who is slow to anger quiets contention." (Proverbs 15:18, ESV)*

❖ *"Whoever is slow to anger has great understanding." (Proverbs 14:29, ESV)*

❖ *Let all bitterness and wrath and anger and clamor and slander be put away from you, along with malice. Be kind to one another, tenderhearted, forgiving one another, as God in Christ forgave you." (Ephesians 4:31-32, ESV)*

❖ *"A man of wrath stirs up strife, and one given to anger causes much transgression." (Proverbs 29:22, ESV)*

Now, we see the consequences and outcomes of allowing your anger to control you. This spirit ends up being passed down through the generations because no one ever takes the time to deal and heal from it.

Rebellion

Rebellion is an action or process of resisting authority, control, or convention. It's defiance, disobedience, insubordination, or resistance. Rebellion has been a problem since the very beginning in Genesis when God commanded Adam to eat from any tree in the garden except for the tree of the knowledge of good and evil. If he did, he would surely die. Eve ate the fruit under the sneaky co-ercion of the serpent and then shared it with her husband, Adam. And just look at the consequences of the sin of rebellion. They all got in trouble.

Because the serpent allowed Satan to use his body to get to Eve, the serpent was cursed to crawl on his belly and to eat dust for the rest of his life, and he and his offspring would know great hostility between women in the future. His curse was self-inflicted because he brought all this trouble onto himself.

Eve was cursed with multiplied pain during childbirth which opened up future generations of women to feel the sting of her rebellion. Not to mention Adam and Eve were husband and wife, for the two are one now.

Adam was not necessarily cursed himself, but struggle was brought upon him. God cursed the ground to make it difficult to provide food for his family. The ground produced only thorns and thistles. Before their rebellion, everything was provided and freely given to them. Now he had to work through extra hard labor by farming the land. Matthew 6:33 (KJV) says, "But seek ye first the kingdom of God, and his righteousness; and all these things shall be added unto you." We have to keep our minds on God and not be steered in our directions.

From the story of Adam and Eve, you learn that your actions of rebellion have consequences not only for you, but also for your husband, your wife, your kids, and generations down the line. The enemy will always try to convince you that if something looks good, then it must be from God. That's not always the case, but is actually the time when your discernment skills come into play. Sometimes, your disobedience may be causing consequences to come upon you and your family. Keep in mind that every ungodly thing we do has a consequence and draws us further away from the Father.

❖ *"But your iniquities have made a separation between you and your God, and your sins have hidden His face from you so that He does not hear." (Isaiah 59:2, ESV)*

Fear was at the root of Saul's rebellion and ultimately caused him to lose the throne and his kingdom (1 Samuel 15:23-24). He had one job to do, and that was to destroy the Amalekites and everything they had, but for whatever reason, he decided to keep their king and some of the animals. He thought they would be good sacrificial burnt offerings. He was told that obedience is better than sacrifice, rebellion is as bad as the sin of witchcraft, and stubbornness is as bad as worshiping idols.

"Because you have rejected the word of the Lord, He has also rejected you from being king," Samuel told Saul (1 Samuel 15: 23, ESV). What a huge blow. You can lose everything just because you want to do things your way and not follow God's path. His path is better anyway. He knows the plans He has for us. They lead to prosperity and good health. He wants nothing but good things for us, so why do we still want to go down our own path? Hebrews 3:17-19 says that the people Moses led out of Egypt turned against God and rebelled. Those who sin are actually rebellious against God because they are going against His word.

❖ *"And if you faithfully obey the voice of the Lord your God, being careful to do all His commandments that I command you today, the Lord your God will set you high above all the nations of the earth. And all these blessings shall come upon you and overtake you, if you obey the voice of the Lord your God." (Deuteronomy 28:1-2, ESV)*

- *"If you love me, you will keep my commandments." (John 14:15, ESV)*

- *"But Peter and the apostles answered, we must obey God rather than men." (Acts 5:29, ESV)*

- *"Children, obey your parents in everything, for this pleases the Lord." (Colossians 3:20, ESV)*

- *"They refused to obey and were not mindful of the wonders that you performed among them, but they stiffened their neck and appointed a leader to return to their slavery in Egypt. But you are a God ready to forgive, gracious and merciful, slow to anger and abounding in steadfast love, and did not forsake them." (Nehemiah 9:17, ESV)*

Declaration Prayer

Lord, help my heart to forgive everyone who has hurt me. I bless them with the love of Christ. Forgive anyone in my bloodline and myself if we have caused harm emotionally or physically to any person. Every spirit of rebellion, hatred, spite, violence, murder, rage, bitterness, strife, and hostility, I renounce you by the power of Jesus Christ. I bring into captivity every rebellious thought and re-place it with the word of God. Any out of order spirit is cast down in the Name of Jesus. Healing and deliverance is mine. I trust and believe that I will always be wise and full of discernment to recognize the schemes of the enemy. I handle every situation just as Jesus would. Great is my composure and peace is mine. I will not fail, but will set my face like flint and stand to do what is right when tempted with anger or rebellion. My bloodline is cleansed in the Name of Jesus!

CHAPTER 5

Generational Chaos and Turmoil

❖ *"For God is not a God of disorder, but of peace as in all the meeting of God's holy people." (1 Corinthians 14:33, NLT)*

As mentioned earlier, when evil spirits are allowed in, they come in, and their plan is to stay for as long as they are allowed. They want to dig deep and penetrate hard. A major goal in their plan is to start as much turmoil and chaos as possible. Have you ever heard someone say things, such as "If it's not one thing, it's another"? Well, that is exactly what will happen because there is power in what we say. The enemy is listening to every word that we speak from our mouths and is preparing plans of sabotage to enter and destroy our lives.

Do you have family members who always have some type of situation going on? Or maybe it's you that has the ongoing issues and problems taking place: car always breaking down; or you're always getting into an accident; always having relationship drama; always fighting and arguing with someone at home, work, or public places.

You change jobs three or four times a year because you do not know how to serve as an employee and are always starting mess. You may even have major money problems or lack thereof, legal issues, church drama, and/or addictions that run rapid in your life. There is no sense of stability or peace in your life. Does this sound like you? Or maybe it is someone you know. It has become a normal dysfunction so much so you hate to pick up the phone when they call because there's always so much going on in their lives. I'm sure it's overwhelming for you and the people they are connected to. Could it be that they do not rest in God? Or could it be that you are not resting in God if similar occurrences are happening in your life?

Spirits of chaos come to distract us and steal our peace of mind. Chaos clutters our minds and has us thinking all kinds of craziness and overloading it with worry and discord. Scripture tells us that we are to be "Casting down imaginations and every high thing that exalteth itself against the knowledge of God, and bringing into captivity every thought to the obedience of Christ." (1 Corinthians 10:5, KJV). God is calling us to be in constant communion with Him. Trusting in Him and not trying to do things or fix things on our own just because the pressure is on us.

Many times, we bring the problems and chaos on ourselves by the bad decisions and choices we make. We do not reach out to God and ask His permission in regard to the important decisions we need to make. We don't ask for guidance or confirmation about our daily tasks or life changes. I've witnessed people change jobs, move to different states, and even marry folks, but they never consulted God about first. The end results were dead ends full of regret and turmoil. There wasn't any type of acceleration or increase that occurred in their lives, and they wondered why. It's because God never told them to do choose that direction. They did not consult with Him first.

But, even when we bring on the problems ourselves, God can make it work for our good and turn situations around. Abraham and Sarah's relationship was so messy, but their promise child still came. He that began a good work in you will complete it. Even the craziest of situations can be our set up. When God has His hand upon you, you will continue to excel. Trouble won't last always, and you will win in every area of your life. You will excel and keep going from glory to glory to glory, and people will recognize the God in your life, but you must seek and trust Him in every area.

That's just what God wants. He wants to restore order where there is dysfunction; stability where things are unstable; freedom and deliverance from bondage, and any other chaotic or life altering behaviors and habits that have gripped your bloodline. You will have a bloodline full of peace and rest; a bloodline that will wash all the junk and craziness out, and fill it with His divine order. He can help you through to live a life in His ways, but you have to want the change and the new direction. You have to want it bad enough not to pass anymore junk down in your family. Remember, the Lord is our solid rock; therefore, we can stand firm knowing that we are stable in Him, reconciled in Him, resting and living in peace and freedom from every single piece of bondage and disorder.

❖ *"But all things should be done decently and in order." (1 Corinthians 14:40, ESV)*

❖ *"Like a city that is broken down and without walls [leaving it un-protected] is a man who has no self-control over his spirit [and sets himself up for trouble]." (Proverbs 25:28, AMP)*

❖ *"You will keep in perfect peace those whose minds are steadfast, be-cause they trust in you." (Isaiah 26:3, KJV)*

❖ *"Now may the Lord of peace himself give you peace at all times in every way. The Lord be with you all." (2 Thessalonians 3:16, ESV)*

❖ *"And the effect of righteousness will be peace, and the result of righteousness will be quietness and confident trust forever. Then my people will live in a peaceful surrounding, and in secure dwellings and in undisturbed resting places." (Isaiah 32:17-18, AMP)*

❖ *"For He himself is our peace…" (Ephesians 2:14, ESV)*

❖ *"Finally, brothers, whatever is true, whatever is honorable, whatever is just, whatever is pure, whatever is lovely, whatever is commendable—if there is any excellence, if there is anything worthy of praise, think about these things…and the God of peace will be with you." (Philippians 4:8-9, ESV)*

Declaration Prayer

Peace be unto me and my bloodline. Great is my peace and great composure. I bind every lie, plot or plan, chaotic situation or circumstance, and spirit of sabotage from the enemy that comes to bring distractions and discouragement in my life. I speak alignment to areas that are out of order in my bloodline. Thank you for being my calm and comfort. Teach me your ways, oh God. I receive your peace that surpasses my understanding. I plead the blood of Jesus over me and ask for your hand to always guide and direct me to make the best decisions possible in Jesus' Name.

CHAPTER 6

Generational Fear

Fear and Worry

F ear lies to you and tells you that you can't do something that God has already marked down and planned for you to complete. Fear places torment on the inside of you to hold you back and halt your God-ordained assignments. It makes you believe that you are not good enough and makes up excuses as to why you can't do what was placed in your heart. How many times have you talked yourself out of achieving something because of fear? Rather, it was because of lack of resources, times, money, connections or courage. "Oh, I'm not smart enough; I'll never be able to afford that house or get that job", but the word of God says, "I can do all things through Christ who strengtheneth me" (Philippians 4:13, KJV).

When you fear, you are trusting in the things that you see, and your faith is weak. Fear of failure demonstrates your lack of hope and trust in our Father. People have fear about their future, their money, their marriage, and their jobs. It keeps them up at night and goes as far as making them ill with sicknesses and diseases. However, there is an answer. The bible tells us that we are to cast our cares upon the Father for He cares for us (1 Peter 5:7). I had to learn this myself.

I used to be so quick to pick up the phone and call a girlfriend before calling on the one and only who could truly fix my troubles. My trust was in hearing my friends tell me everything was going to be all right, them praying for me, and passing along scripture instead of me trusting that God could and would move mountains in my life and work out every circumstance that concerned me.

I have learned to build my own faith. I learned to have faith smaller than a mustard seed. I learned to pray the scriptures over my own self. I learned to talk to God FIRST because He was not going to lead me astray. Our faith must lie within Him and not others. Others can't heal you, and others sure can't make your fears go away. But Jesus can.

Failure

What's the root of your fear? Is it failure and depression? Are you constantly worried about what others think of you or even your family? These are people pleasers who strive for ungodly perfection, but striving for perfection is different than striving for a spirit of excellence because perfection can sometimes be rooted in pride. According to Proverbs 29:25, when you trust in God, you are safe from the snare of people.

You don't have to worry about what others think about you because you are concerned with the Father, and you know how He sees you. You are the apple of His eye, and your concerns are His concerns. Because we are not to worry or fear, then we certainly don't have to worry about failure. There's no failure in God. His plans are far better than we could ever think or imagine, and fear, worry, failure, and depression aren't in those plans.

Depression

Normally, the spirit of depression invades those who lack self-worth and security. They have been abandoned or verbally and physically abused. They feel that they worthless, and their self-worth is in how others see them as people, so they look to get compliments or accolades of achievement from others in order to stay encourage, uplifted, or motivated. If not, they feel rejected and unwanted. Their self-esteem is low, and the devil comes into their minds to make them believe they are nothing and life isn't even worth living for. They have been rejected, are lonely, and hurt by others who they thought loved them.

Possibly, they have been humiliated, ostracized, and manipulated. They have feelings of being abandoned, alienated, isolated, and are unwilling to forgive. Their goal is to feel loved by others, but true love comes only from and through the Father. He walks us in His love, and in His presence, we find comfort from all of our insecurities.

Or maybe something didn't work out the way they thought it would. There may have been a broken relationship, a family member or close friend who passed away, or a business deal that went wrong and they lost everything. Whatever the circumstance; whether depression or grief, it can hit you like a ton of bricks with a load that is too heavy for you to carry alone. If you know someone that struggles with depression, pray for them, esteem them with the love of Christ, and share God's word to help them through the difficult time.

❖ *"But you, Lord, are a shield about me, my glory, and the lifter of my head." (Psalm 3:3, ESV)*

❖ *"There is no fear in love, but perfect love casts out fear. For fear has to do with punishment, and whoever fears has not been perfected in love." (1 John 4:18, ESV)*

❖ *"For you are my lamp, O Lord, and my God lightens my darkness." (2 Samuel 22:29, ESV)*

❖ *"For God gave us a spirit not of fear but of power and love and self-control." (2 Timothy 1:7, ESV)*

❖ *"So we say with confidence, The Lord is my helper; I will not be afraid. What can mere people do to me?" (Hebrews 13:6, NLT)*

❖ *"…casting all your anxieties on Him, because He cares for you." (1 Peter 5:7, ESV)*

❖ *"See, God has come to save me. I will trust in Him and not be afraid. The Lord God is my strength and my song; he has given me victory." (Isaiah 12:2, NLT)*

❖ *"…but they who wait for the Lord shall renew their strength; they shall mount up with wings like eagles; they shall run and not be weary; they shall walk and not faint." (Isaiah 40:31, ESV)*

❖ *"It is the Lord who goes before you. He will be with you. He will not leave you or forsake you. Do not fear or be dismayed." (Deuteronomy 31:8, ESV)*

❖ *""…Weeping may endure for a night, but joy cometh in the morning." (Psalm 30:5, KJV)*

❖ *"But immediately Jesus spoke to them, saying, 'Take heart; it is I. Do not be afraid.'" (Matthew 14:27, ESV)*

❖ *"Peace I leave with you; my peace I give to you. Not as the world gives do I give to you. Let not your hearts be troubled, neither let them be afraid." (John 14:27, ESV)*

❖ *"Answer me quickly, O Lord! My spirit fails! Hide not your face from me, lest I be like those who go down to the pit. Let me hear in the morning of your steadfast love, for in you I trust. Make me know the way I should go, for to you I lift up my soul." (Psalm 143:7-9, ESV)*

❖ *"Say to those who have an anxious heart, Be strong; fear not! Behold, your God will come with vengeance, with the recompense of God. He will come and save you." (Isaiah 35:4, ESV)*

❖ *"Why are you cast down, O my soul, and why are you in turmoil within me? Hope in God; for I shall again praise Him, my salvation and my God." (Psalm 42:11, ESV)*

❖ *"Have I not commanded you? Be strong and courageous. Do not be frightened, and do not be dismayed, for the Lord your God is with you wherever you go." (Joshua 1:9, ESV)*

❖ *"I waited patiently for the Lord to help me, and He turned to me and heard my cry. He lifted me out of the pit of despair, out of the mud and mire; He set my feet on solid ground and steadied me as I walked along. He has given me a new song to sing, a hymn of praise to our God. Many will see what He has done and be amazed. They will put their trust in the Lord." (Psalm 40:1-3, NLT)*

❖ *"So don't worry about tomorrow, for tomorrow will bring its own worries. Today's trouble is enough for today." (Matthew 6:34, NLT)*

❖ *"…Fear not, for I have redeemed you; I have called you by name, you are mine." (Isaiah 43:1, ESV)*

❖ *"Even though I walk through the valley of the shadow of death, I will fear no evil, for you are with me; your rod and your staff, they comfort me." (Psalm 23:4, ESV)*

Declaration Prayer

I thank you, Father, for giving me the spirit of power and love and of a sound mind. I am free from worry, stress, depression, anxiety, failure, and fear. You have delivered me from the power of darkness and translated me into the kingdom of the son of His love according to Colossians 1:13. I will not fear the terrors by night nor the arrow that flies by day, but will stand by faith on the word of the Lord. I silence fear near me and let faith arise. I take every thought captive that is not of you and make it obedient to Christ Jesus. Fear, worry, anxiety, failure, and depression, Let Me GO! I trust the hand of the Almighty and that He will guide and keep me in all my ways. Father, I trust in your plans and promises and know that you are a God who cannot lie. I surrender my future and put it in your hands. I have the mind of Christ Jesus, and I draw closer to you daily in the Name of Jesus.

CHAPTER 7

Generational Family Sickness and Illnesses

❖ *"…With His stripes, we are healed." (Isaiah 53:5, KJV)*

Infirmities attack generational bloodlines to keep us bound, weak, and distracted throughout generations. We have to pray and believe God for health and prosperity in order to be strong and build the kingdom of God. The Lord is our strength, and according to His word, we are healed. And for those of us who truly believe that scripture, there is no sickness or disease can keep us down. We actually slap the enemy in the face because it draws us closer to God when we trust what His word says about us. We seek His face even the more; we are on our knees even the more; and others are interceding for us even the more. We are opening up our mouths and proclaiming the name of the Lord that is above all to be our healer and our way maker. You are surrounded by people who begin to decree and resist the powers of sickness, and what happens when we resist that sickness, IT FLEES (James 4:7).

Infirmities are not only things such as cancer, diabetes, and viruses, just to name a few, but they are also alcoholism, drugs, addictions, disorders, mental illnesses, and physical disabilities. Whatever the infirmity, you can be healed and delivered. It is God's will for all of us to be in good health and prosper. Being healthy is defined as well, fine, fit, and not diseased. Everything in your body functions the way it was created to function. It is the enemy that tries to come and take that from us.

"The thief comes only to steal and kill and destroy. I came that they may have life and have it abundantly." (John 10:10, ESV)

The devil will use fear to grip you into thinking you will never get well and overload your mind with thoughts of premature death. You speak things over your life like, "Well, since Daddy had it, I'll probably get it too". No, the devil is a liar. No, you will not. It doesn't matter how many generations have had the illness or the addiction, it will end with you. Stay consistent in prayer and vigilant because the enemy will try whatever he can to get you down. Always remember to guard your spirit and don't give the enemy legal entry because sin, disobedience, fear, stress, anxiety, unforgiveness, and many others can cause illnesses as well.

The good news is that we have power and dominion over Satan through the blood of Jesus. When we realize and operate in the fullness of what God's word says about us and what He did on the cross, we will conquer the giants in our lives every single time. The devil doesn't stand a chance against the wonder working power of Jesus Christ.

- ❖ *"And they have conquered him by the blood of the Lamb and by the word of their testimony…" (Revelation 12:11, ESV)*

- ❖ *"But the Lord said, 'My grace is all you need. Only when you are weak can everything be done completely by my power.' So I will gladly boast about my weaknesses. Then Christ's power can stay in me." (2 Corinthians 12:9, ERV)*

- ❖ *"Is anyone among you sick? Let him call for the elders of the church, and let them pray over him, anointing him with oil in the name of* the Lord. And the prayer of faith will save the one who is sick, and the Lord will raise him up. And if he has committed sins, he will be forgiven." (James 5:14-15, ESV)

❖ "He said, 'If you listen carefully to the Lord your God and do what is right in His eyes, if you pay attention to his commands and keep all His decrees, I will not bring on you any of the diseases I brought on the Egyptians, for I am the Lord who heals you.'" (Exodus 15:26, ESV)

❖ "You shall serve the Lord your God, and He will bless your bread and your water, and I will take sickness away from among you. (Exodus 23:25, NLT)

❖ "Yet it was our weakness He carried; it was our sorrows that weighed Him down. And we thought His troubles were a punishment from God, a punishment for His own sins! But He was pierced for our rebellion, crushed for our sins. He was beaten so we could be whole. He was whipped so we could be healed." (Isaiah 53:4-5, NLT)

❖ "For I will restore health to you and your wounds I will heal, declares the Lord, because they have called you an outcast: 'It is Zion, for whom no one cares!'" (Jeremiah 30:17, ESV)

❖ "Beloved, I pray that all may go well with you and that you may be in good health, as it goes well with your soul." (3 John 1:2, ESV)

❖ "And my God will supply every need of yours according to His riches in glory in Christ Jesus." (Philippians 4:19, NLT)

Declaration Prayer

I pray for relief of sickness and disease from my body and those within my bloodline. Forgive us from our iniquities and heal our disease. Only you can do it, Father, for you are the Lord who heals.

Just like the woman with the issue of blood, I reach out to you God for complete healing. You touched her because she touched you. Place your delivering hands on me and never let me go. I bind any lie from the devil and renounce every lie spoken against my health. I put my health in your hands, and I decree that I will prosper in all things and be in good health, just as my soul prospers. Every area of my body functions the way it was created to function, and by your stripes, Father, I am healed in the Name of Jesus!

CHAPTER 8

🔓

Generational Jealousy, Strife, and Unforgiveness

❖ *"And do not give the devil an opportunity [to lead you into sin by holding a grudge, or nurturing anger, or harboring resentment, or cultivating bitterness]." (Ephesians 4:27, AMP)*

Bitterness and strife are strongly connected to unforgiveness and unforgiveness gives birth to anger and hatred. Hatred is a strong word and is extremely harsh, but the reality is most people don't even realize they carry that much aggression in their hearts towards someone. Their minds race with plots of revenge against the person who has hurt them. They end up being envious, jealous, and then strife forms in the midst.

Jealousy and envy are rooted in fear and pride. It comes from a sense of inadequacy within that turns deeper into strife. The enemy stirs up strife, envy and unforgiveness in the hearts of God's people and will keep cultivating them in order to make the issues harder to remove. Maybe someone lied on you, schemed, and got the job you wanted. Maybe he stole your girlfriend or had an affair with your wife. Or more seriously, a drunk driver hit the car your child and spouse were in which resulted in them passing away. Those are some hard pills to swallow, and only God can bring the person to forgive.

❖ *"And whenever you stand praying, forgive, if you have anything against anyone, so that your Father also who is in heaven may forgive you your trespasses." (Mark 11:25, ESV)*

The bible speaks about strife and warns that we should avoid it in Proverbs 20:3 (ESV), "Avoiding a fight is a mark of honor; only fools insist on quarreling." You think you are right, and the other person thinks they are right. Disagreements may occur, and personalities may clash, but avoiding strife is always best. Otherwise, it can become a never ending dramatized fight. Strife destroys unity within families, co-workers on jobs, and members in the churches. Love cannot exist if strife is present. So, overcome evil with good by cutting it by the neck. Go out your way to show love towards others. The bible says that we are to love God and our neighbor (Matthew 22:37-39).

Often times, family members stop speaking because of offenses or times when they were trying to prove a point that didn't go the way they planned. One day leads to weeks, weeks lead to months, and before you know it, you haven't spoken to the person in years. If we have a problem with someone, we are to go and make things right immediately. We are to be quick to forgive and even ask for forgiveness. If not, generations of anger, strife, jealously, and envy will be passed down. Those spirits get stronger and stronger the longer they are allowed to fester. I once heard Bishop George Davis say, "Christians need to learn how to have a short memory". I agree, but that phrase is also for the unbelievers as well. It will enable us to forgive and forget quickly.

We will never be able to pursue and accomplish our assignments if we are always in conflict with others or jealous of our neighbor. The very person who you just decided to stop speaking to could have been your miracle or the open door to something God was trying to do in your life. The person may have come your way to teach you about patience, love, trust, and faithfulness. Don't get held up and delay your promise. We are created in His image, and the Lord hates strife so do not get involved and twisted up in it.

Many times, disconnections and breaks occur within the body of Christ and in personal relationships because we expect way more than what people are actually able to give and provide us. People can be spoiled to have things their way instead of following proper order and alignment. Selfish desires and manipulating spirits are then revealed.

On the other hand, being on one accord and united will create and form a bond of power that the enemy cannot overpower. It's important to not let the enemy into our lives and relationships to bring discord, breaches, and offenses or allow the orphan spirit to dissipate the connected spiritual atmosphere that is intertwined within God's people.

It's also important to make every effort to move in peace with those around you, especially leaders. They are your earthly visionaries who assist in biblical instruction and guidance. But so many times, people encounter church hurt that is sometimes caused by their own disobedience to proper alignment. They were out of order. With those in your sphere, you want to have a peaceful covering of order, unity, bond, and blessings that creates an unshakeable team. When you love, all the other problems fall down and die. How do you handle situations that don't go your way?

❖ *"Most important of all, continue to show deep love for each other, for love covers a multitude of sins." (1 Peter 4:8, NLT)*

❖ *"Repay no one evil for evil, but give thought to do what is honorable in the sight of all. If possible, so far as it depends on you, live peaceably* with all. Beloved, never avenge yourselves, but leave it to the wrath of God, for it is written, 'Vengeance is mine, I will repay,' says the Lord…..Do not be overcome by evil, but overcome evil with good." (Romans 12:17-21, ESV)

❖ "Only by pride cometh contention: but with the well advised is wisdom." (Proverbs 13:10, KJV)

❖ "What causes quarrels and what causes fights among you? Is it not this, that your passions are at war within you? You desire and do not have, so you murder. You covet and cannot obtain, so you fight and quarrel. You do not have, because you do not ask." (James 4:1-2, ESV)

❖ "Be kind to one another, tenderhearted, forgiving one another, as God in Christ forgave you." (Ephesians 4:32 ESV)

❖ "A soft answer turns away wrath, but a harsh word stirs up anger." (Proverbs 15:1, ESV)

❖ "Bearing with one another and, if one has a complaint against another, forgiving each other; as the Lord has forgiven you, so you also must forgive." (Colossians 3:13, ESV)

❖ "Hated stirs up strife, but love covers all offenses." (Proverbs 10:12, ESV)

Declaration Prayer

Lord, I forgive anyone who has hurt me. Let me always be quick to forgive and to bless them with the love of Christ. I will follow by your example and love one another. Open up the hearts of those whom myself or my ancestors have hurt and caused division and strife with. Enable them to forgive me and those in my bloodline. Restore broken relationships that were caused by jealously, conflicts, unforgiveness, ill motives, and bitterness. I cling to the heart of love and peace. I declare that I have wisdom in dealing with difficult people and operate in the spirit of love and order. I declare that I am happy and proud of the things you have blessed me with and desire only the things of you Lord. I do not covenant anything from anyone else and I rest in my Savior who brings me my happiness and wholeness. I am complete with nothing missing and nothing broken In Jesus' Name.

CHAPTER 9

Generational Pride

❖ *"An high look and a proud heart and the plowing of the wicked is sin." (Proverbs 21:4, KJV)*

Being prideful is a sin that the Lord hates and is an abomination unto Him according to Proverbs 16:5. If you don't know, an abomination is defined as a thing that causes disgust; an atrocity, a disgrace, or evil. In the book of Exodus, the Lord asked Pharaoh, "How long will you refuse to humble yourself before me? Let my people go, so that they may worship me. If you refuse to let them go, I will bring locusts into your country tomorrow." When you allow deep stubborn pride to get into your life, sometimes God has to intervene; and it's gotten pretty bad when God has to warn you severely.

All sin, including pride, can cause you to lose out on many good things in your life. Generations suffer because of prideful mistakes and sins of our forefathers. When not recognized and defeated, they cause pain in our current lives and pain for future generations. We know the scripture that says, "Too much pride will destroy you. You are better off to be humble and poor than to get rich from what you take by force." (Proverbs 16:18, CEV). Well, pride is what keeps you from doing what you should do, such as humbling yourself to the Father when you've been too stubborn or when you know you are not well and need help in a certain area of your life.

Pride is when you think no one is right except for you or feel that you are the best in an area or ability.

I recall being an office assistant at 19 years of age and was laid off because the business wasn't doing well. I remember telling one of my coworkers, "He's not going to find someone that does everything I do and as good as me". My coworker looked at me and said, "Don't ever think you can't be replaced." Those words broke my little heart, but they were the truth.

People can think they are the best singer, dancer, writer, preacher, teacher, or supervisor, when the reality is it's not them at all. They didn't give themselves those abilities, gifts or anointing; these come from God, and the gifts that we receive are to serve others. God's word tells us who we are in Christ.

Pride is when you put more trust and faith in your abilities as opposed to God and His abilities. It's your job to cultivate the gifting God has placed on the inside of you so that it will bring Him glory. The bible also says that whatever we do, we are to do it wholeheartedly unto the Lord and not for human masters (Colossians 3:23). The truth is, no one will flat out admit to being prideful because at times, it can be hard to identify within your own self.

Areas of Pride

- ♣ Boasting and bragging about your accomplishments

- ♣ Not admitting when you are wrong

- ♣ Attention seeking and taking credit for everything even when others helped

- ♣ Thinking you have a closer relationship with God than others. Often times, this is more common in older people, but age doesn't always mean wiser.

- ♣ Stubbornness

- ♣ Fault finding and having a harsh spirit toward others

- ♣ Name dropping (you don't know those people)

- ♣ Looking down on others thinking you are better

- ♣ Always defensive or taking offense

- ♣ Selfish behaviors

Additionally, how do you carry on relationships and conversations with others? Is the conversation all about you? There's a difference between sharing some good news, especially if you are giving God the glory; but it's another thing having a showoff or boasting spirit. Boasting is defined as talk with excessive pride and self-satisfaction about one's achievements, possessions, or abilities.

Or have you ever shared something so amazing that happened in your life with someone and they responded by telling you what happened to them and or what they received too! The person never really acknowledged your blessing or may have even changed the subject completely. Kind of like a tit for tat conversation only they are "tatting" on everything you say. They're never really happy for anyone who they see excelling and are always wanting "one up" on others. In some families, undercover pride may be a reality that is sneaky to unfold and come out. Celebrations are downsized, no one really supports others, and the love seems so distant. Stay humble by having a true love for God and others. As stated earlier, when you love, all the other problems fall down and die.

❖ *"Above all, keep loving one another earnestly, sine love covers a multitude of sins." (1 Peter 4:8, ESV)*

We must ask God to search our hearts and reveal any forms of pride in our lives so that we can be free and defeat this disease. Prideful people fall, but righteous people rise up high above because they recognize the pitfalls of sin and other fleshly desires that try to hold them down and delay their destinies. Seek God in everything. Ask God to give you eyes like an eagle that you may see yourself clearly so that you will rule over the enemy of pride in Jesus Name.

❖ *"But He gives us more grace. Therefore it says: "God opposes the proud but gives grace to the humble." (James 4:6, ESV)*

❖ *"Humble yourselves, therefore, under the mighty hand of God so that at the proper time He may exalt you, casting all your anxieties on Him, because He cares for you." (1 Peter 5:6, ESV)*

❖ *"Everyone who is arrogant in heart is an abomination to the Lord; be assured, he will not go unpunished." (Proverbs 16:5, ESV)*

❖ *"Humble yourselves in the sight of the Lord, and He shall lift you up." (James 4:10, KJV)*

❖ *"A man's pride shall bring him low: but honour shall uphold the humble in spirit." (Proverbs 29:23, KJV)*

❖ *"and be clothed with humility: for God resisteth the proud, and giveth grace to the humble." (1 Peter 5:5, KJV)*

❖ *"So when you fast, wash your face and make yourself look nice. Then no one will know you are fasting, except your Father, who is with you even in private. He can see what is done in private, and He will reward you." (Matthew 6:17-18, ERV)*

Declaration Prayer

Lord, I come to you with sincere humility. I bind and renounce any spirits of pride that are in operation in my life. I sever the demonic stronghold roots of pride that have attached to me and held me back from receiving the promises of God. I decree my heart is running over and filled to the rim with love and humility. I am graced with humility, and I am clothed and covered with humility. Forgive me and my bloodline as we move forward in trusting you to lift us instead of man. I live in harmony with others, and I represent you in every area of my life. I declare my eyes will always be open to recognize and overcome the spirit of pride in Jesus' Name!

CHAPTER 10

Generational Lying and Word Curses

❖ *"Lying lips are an abomination to the Lord, but those who act faithfully are His delight." (Proverbs 12:22, ESV)*

Of course God would not be happy with those who have lying tongues. It would go against everything that He is. He is the truth and the light (John 14:6). He is a God that cannot lie. If He said something, you'd better believe it will come to past. It's His divine nature to stand and remain in truth, and because we are created in His image and are to set our sights on becoming more like Him daily, we are too. The exact opposite of truth is a lie, and the foundation of lies lives in the father of the lies (Satan). John 8:44 (ESV) says, "You are of your father the devil, and your will is to do your father's desires. He was a murderer from the beginning, and has nothing to do with truth, because there is no truth in him. When he lies, he speaks out of his own character, for he is a liar and the father of lies."

Lying is deceitful and believe it or not is a form of witchcraft because you are manipulating people into thinking something that is really untrue which is against the word of God. There's no such thing as a little white lie. A lie is a lie and causes lasting consequences for you and the people connected to you.

In Genesis 27, Jacob lied to his father, but worse than that, he lied on God. Jacob and Esau's father, Isaac had grown old and could barely see, but he wanted to bless his first born Esau before he died. He told Esau to kill an animal and prepare the food for him to eat, and then he would bless him before he died.

Their mother Rebekah overheard and told Jacob what his father had said. They came up with a plan to deceive Isaac into thinking Jacob was Esau so that Jacob would get the birth right. Lying obviously ran in the family through their bloodline. But anyway, did Jacob not realize what he was doing? Sure, he did. His name means tricky one and sneaky thief. Some may argue that Esau did not care about the birthright in the first place and that Jacob is the one that really wanted the blessings of God. Either way, Jacob lied.

Sometimes we want things so badly; we are willing to sacrifice relationships with the people we love. Jacob lied without even thinking twice about doing it. He betrayed his brother and dishonored his father and the Lord. Once lies start, you have to continue in them just to keep the lies going, and that's too much work. I've been there and done that. If you have to lie about something, you already know it's not good for you. Lying ruins your character and you become seen as untrustworthy and foolish. Everything you say and do becomes fickle. Scripture in Proverbs 6 says that the Lord hates a lying tongue and that it is considered an abomination to him.

Furthermore, Jacob's family's lying spirit didn't stop there. Later, Labon (Rebekah's brother) lied to Jacob and tricked him into sleeping with Leah when he really only wanted Rachel. Years later, Jacob was deceitful with Labon by not telling him he was leaving with his family. What a lying bunch of folks with selfish motives.

Bad decisions wrapped in lies take you on rollercoaster rides that you never wanted to go on in the first place. Participating in gossip, backbiting, and other sins of the tongue are just the same as using your tongue to do evil against others. Scripture says, "Let no corrupting talk come out of your mouths, but only such as is good for building up, as fits the occasion, that it may give grace to those who hear."(Ephesians 4:29, ESV)

Watch what you say. When you are truly genuine about pleasing the Father and doing what's right, nothing can convince you otherwise. Your desire should be to live a true authentic life and not have to lie about anything. Even if you have a past that would be looked upon as bad, who cares? You don't have to lie about it, for it's a part of your testimony. Your response should be, " Yes, I did whatever, but let me tell you how God came into my life, wrapped me in His arms, and cleaned me up to do His works." My point is God is our only source of truth because He is truth. He protects and covers us from the outside forces that try to trip us up.

You cannot let anyone speak any and everything over your life, even if it is someone close to you or in your family. They may say, "You are going to be just like your daddy in jail and on drugs." No, that's when you have to open up your mouth and respond, "No I'm not. I'm just like my heavenly Father!" Reverse it and cancel it!

These are word curses that take root in families. People are struggling with things that were spoken over their lives by their mothers, fathers, aunt, uncles, and even pastors. You grew up believing and receiving what they spoke, and it became so in your life. Don't allow people to lie on your life, plant word curses, and diminish who God created you to be. You have to speak life even when it doesn't look like it and when others don't see it either.

It was second nature for me to correct my children or someone I would be having a conversation with. I was quick to say, "Oh, yes, you will get that job" or "No, you are healed in the Name of Jesus." I even corrected myself when thoughts came to get me down. I quoted the scripture and spoke the truth over my life instead of the lies of the enemy, and you must do the same.

The enemy would love for you to believe his lies. He would love for you to believe that you'll never be anointed, never kick the addiction, never get out the hood, never get that house, and never get that new position. He wants us to stay bound and trapped in old ways of thinking so he plants discouragement, low confidence, compromise, fear, and distrust in God's word. He wants you to stay a wimp in the spirit. But to every lie that the enemy says, the word of God says the complete opposite (the truth).

- ➤ You're not smart enough – 1 Corinthians 1:30 says you have wisdom

- ➤ You're all alone – Hebrews 13:5 says God will never leave you

- ➤ You can't do it – Philippians 4:13 says you can do all things

- ➤ I'm afraid to step out – 2 Timothy 1:7 says God has not given you the spirit of fear

- ➤ I'm not loved – John 3:16 says God loves everyone in the world

- ❖ *"You will destroy those who tell lies. The Lord detests murderers and deceivers." (Psalm 5:6, NLT)*

- ❖ *"He who works deceit shall not dwell within my house; he who tells lies shall not tarry in my sight." (Psalm 101:7, KJV)*

❖ *"Death and life are in the power of the tongue, and those who live it will eat its fruit." (Proverbs 18:21, ESV)*

❖ *"You must not testify falsely against your neighbor." (Exodus 20:16, NLT)*

❖ *"Since we have the same spirit of faith according to what has been written, "I believed, and so I spoke, we also believe, and so we also speak." (2 Corinthians 4:13, ESV)*

❖ *"There are six things that the Lord hates, seven are an abomination to Him: haughty eyes, a lying tongue, and hands that shed innocent blood, a heart that devises wicked plans, feet that make haste to run to evil, a false witness who breathes out lies and one who sows discord among brothers." (Proverbs 6:16,19, ESV)*

❖ *"The tongue is like a fire. It is a world of evil among the parts of our body. It spreads its evil through our whole body and starts a fire that influences all of life. It gets this fire from hell." (James 3:6, ERV)*

❖ *"He is the Rock, His deeds are perfect. Everything He does is just and fair. He is a faithful God who does no wrong; how just and up-right He is!" (Deuteronomy 32:4, NLT)*

❖ *"In hope of eternal life, which God, that cannot lie, promised before the world began." (Titus 1:2, KJV)*

❖ *"And stop lying to each other. You have given up your old way of life with its habits." (Colossians 3:9, CEV)*

❖ *"So stop telling lies. Let us tell our neighbors the truth, for we are all parts of the same body." (Ephesians 4:25, NLT)*

❖ *"A false witness will not go unpunished, and he who breathes lies will not escape." (Proverbs 19:5, ESV)*

❖ *"But the cowards, unbelievers, the corrupt, murderers, the immoral, those who practice witchcraft, idol worshipers, and all liars—their fate is in the fiery lake of burning sulfur. This is the second death."* (Revelations 21:8, NLT)

❖ *"The godly hate lies; the wicked cause shame and disgrace."* (Proverbs 13:5, NLT)

Declaration Prayer

Lord, forgive me of any ill and ungodly curses that I have spoken out of my mouth. I renounce and rebuke the corrupt things spoken by my ancestors. Catch, cancel, and cast those words back to the pit of hell. I speak and declare life and not death over my bloodline. I let no corrupt words proceed from my mouth, and I speak only good words that edify and minister grace to the hearers. I will not lie or be deceitful, but will only speak the truth in love. You are the God of truth, and I will honor you with the things I do and say at all times.

CHAPTER 11

Generational Divorce and the Unmarried

There are a lot of people believing God for a godly marriage. They have a deep longing and desire to have companionship, and there's nothing wrong with having that desire. Personally, for some reason, I used to feel embarrassed as a single woman to share with someone that I desired to be a wife. It felt like it was a walk of shame. But as I grew in Christ, I learned that God's timing is never wrong. I learned patience and how to prepare for the future. I was determined to be a godly wife before I was even found by my husband. However, at times, it seemed hopeless as I looked around within my family and there weren't a lot of examples of fruitful marriages.

My family has had their share of difficulties in the area of marriage. Some have married and divorced a few times, and the rest have never been married and like to jump from relationship after relationship fast and very deep without the marriage commitment. I wondered if something took place within my bloodline that caused marriages to be nonexistent or to dissolve quickly into divorce. It could very well be a curse that draws you to seek flesh and jump into commitments when is not God's wil. These choices can put an extreme delay your destiny.

Jesus spoke to a Samaritan woman who came to draw water from the well that He was resting near. Jesus asked her for a drink of water and they began a conversation about "living water". "Go and get your husband", Jesus told her. "I don't have a husband," the woman replied. Jesus said, "You're right! You don't have a husband for you have had five husbands, and you aren't even married to the man you're living with now. You certainly spoke the truth!"

I've noticed that we sometimes want what we want right now, not thinking of what might come later. We want what we want without seeking God first, even before the first date. We need to seek His "living waters" (that never run dry) instead of searching for love in all the wrong places.

Preparation and order is crucial before beginning anything. If you're single now, what kind of prayers are you praying for your future spouse? Are you preparing yourself for marriage? Are you a husband right now? Are you a wife right now? Are you ready to be found or to find that someone? While single, you have lots of time to groom yourself. Think about Esther. She prepared herself for an entire year before she went to be with the King. In 1 Corinthians 7:34 (NLT) we read, "…a woman who is no longer married or has never been married can be devoted to the Lord and holy in body and in spirit. But a married woman has to think about her earthly responsibilities and how to please her husband."

You have the time to cultivate yourself during your single season. Being single is not a burden, but a gift from God. Do you know what the bible says about being a godly mate? It's an amazing experience to be in prayer for your own character development and then transition into the married life. It saves on a lot of trouble and drama when two whole people are joined together and become one. Additionally, don't ever let someone tell you that pre-marital counseling is a waste of time. It absolutely is not and is extremely beneficial. As a matter of fact, if a pastor or minister says he will marry you without pre-marital counseling, this should be a red flag that they don't have your best interest at heart because the counseling encourages and inspires both people to follow God's plan for their lives and provides sound counsel.

Many of us want something in a mate that we ourselves do not mirror. We want them to be our rescuer and deliverer. You even have a checklist. "Must have good credit, a degree, a job paying this amount, no drama" and the list goes on. If the tables were turned, would you qualify under these terms? Some people don't care about any standards and marry without thinking twice or asking if it is in God's will for them to marry that person. They rush in quickly only to end in divorce.

Divorce rates are on the rise in the church just as much as in the world. Marriage was the first institution created by God because He said it was not good for man to be alone. God loves marriage and considers it sacred. God hates divorce, probably, because something happens within the marriage where Jesus was not at the center of it. One or both parties stepped out of God's will in the marriage and caused a rift, and an inability formed that prevented them from overcoming the obstacle. Circumstances happen in life, and no marriage is perfect, but God can give you the strength and love towards one another to keep moving forward even when difficulties occur.

For the people who have been through divorced, no matter how many times you have been married, God can still bring you your ordained mate. You might feel like a failure or that you have messed up too many times, but God can bring that someone special into your life. I've seen Him do it for others. Think of the difficulties that could have been avoided if you had sought after God first before you made that decision.

What if you had sought counsel? Do you think you would have gone through with it? Sometimes, we delay our own blessings by doing our own will, but God is a restorer and a healer to things that are broken. Find a way to consistently pray and fight for your spouse TOGETHER.

❖ *"Two are better than one, because they have a good return for their labor. For if either of them falls, the one will lift up his companion. But woe to the one who falls when there is not another to lift him up. Furthermore, if two lie down together they keep warm, but how can one be warm alone?" (Ecclesiastes 4:9-11, NASB)*

❖ *"The man who finds a wife finds a treasure, and he receives favor from the Lord." (Proverbs 18:22, NLT)*

❖ *"For the man who does not love his wife, but divorces her, says the Lord, the God of Israel, covers his garment with violence, says the Lord of hosts. So guard yourselves in your spirit, and do not be faithless." (Malachi 2:16, ESV)*

❖ *"A worthy wife is a crown for her husband, but a disgraceful woman is like cancer in his bones." (Proverbs 12:4, NLT)*

❖ *"The Lord God said, It is not good for the man to be alone. I will make a helper who is just right for him." (Genesis 2:18, NLT)*

❖ *"A wife must put her husband first. This is her duty as a follower of the Lord." (Colossians 3:18-19, CEV)*

❖ *"Let your wife be a fountain of blessings for you. Rejoice in the wife of your youth. She is a loving deer, a graceful doe. Let her breasts satisfy you always. May you always be captivated by her love." (Proverbs 5:18-19, NLT)*

❖ *"I tell you, you can pray for anything, and if you believe that you've received it, it will be yours." (Mark 11:24, NLT)*

❖ *"But there is one thing I want you to know: The head of every man is Christ, the head of woman is man, and the head of Christ is God." (1 Corinthians 11:3, NLT)*

❖ *"Take delight in the Lord, and He will give you your heart's desires." (Psalms 37:4, NLT)*

❖ *"Do not be unequally yoked with unbelievers. For what partnership has righteousness with lawlessness? Or what fellowship has light with darkness?" (2 Corinthians 6:14, ESV)*

Declaration Prayer (For Married Couples)

Father, thank you for my spouse and our godly marriage. Forgive us for not putting you first in all that we do. I pray that our marriage is one of faith, courage, and strength. I believe that you can do the miraculous in our lives. Thank you Lord for making crooked areas line up according to your word. Our minds are renewed, and my spouse and I are clothed with humility, wisdom and support for one another. May the lines of productive communication be opened upon us. I pray we both have a servant's heart toward one another. Lord, our hearts are changed forever as we look to you. Revive our marriage with a fresh fire Father. We keep you first and at the center of everything we do. Together with you, we are a three-stranded cord that cannot be easily broken. The devil will not have my marriage, and the curse of divorce is broken in my bloodline. Turmoil, strife, and mistreatment of any kind, I bind you and replace you with love, joy, peace, patience, kindness, goodness, faithfulness, gentleness and self-control. We have quick forgiving hearts. God's hand is on my marriage In Jesus' Name!

Declaration Prayer (For Singles)

Heavenly Father, equip me as a single person to be prepared for my next phase of married life. Train me up Lord and mold me into a godly spouse. Help me to prepare with purpose so that I will be able to demonstrate unconditional love towards my spouse. Keep me pure and guard my heart during the process. Thank you for granting me wisdom and discernment to make good decisions. Thank you for blessing my future marriage and giving me strength to conquer any obstacles that may come my way In Jesus' Name Amen!

CHAPTER 12

Generational Witchcraft and False Idol Worship

❖ *"When you follow the desires of your sinful nature, the results are very clear: sexual immorality, impurity, lustful pleasures, idolatry, sorcery, hostility, quarreling, jealousy, outburst of anger, selfish ambition, dissension, division, envy, drunkenness, wild parties, and other sins like these. Let me tell you again, as I have before, that anyone living that sort of life will not inherit the kingdom of God."* *(Galatians 5:19-21, NLT)*

Witchcraft

Witchcraft is a demonic technique and practice of magic, especially black magic, the use of spells, and the invocation of spirits. Identifying spirits of witchcraft takes discernment because these spirits can come through common areas of struggles that we wouldn't normally tie them with such as: intimidation, confusion, manipulation, domination, spiritual control, soul ties, deception of fear, pride, jealousy, and other hidden motives. People who participate in these dark rituals sometimes don't even realize they are in communication with demonic forces (to include curses) that work against the spirit of God. These spirits operate as blood sucking forces that attempt to destroy us and our godly bloodline, but the good news is that Jesus has authority over these evil forces, and so do we. We have the power under the blood of Jesus to destroy them in our lives. Through discernment and revelation, we are able identify and get freed from these ungodly spirits. Therefore, Satan must bow and flee.

Jezebel

There is a witchcraft spirit that manifests itself in family bloodlines through seduction and intimacy. Excessive manipulation, control, and the need to be involved in everything and everyone's business are of a Jezebel spirit. "But I have this [charge] against you, that you tolerate the woman Jezebel, who calls herself a prophetess [claiming to be inspired], and she teaches and misleads My bond-servants so that they commit [acts of sexual] immorality and eat food sacrificed to idols. I gave her time to repent [to change her inner self and her sinful way of thinking], but she has no desire to repent of her immorality and refuses to do so." (Revelation 2:20-21, AMP).

In one of Jonas Clark's book entitled *Jezebel*, he says "In the wake of every Jezebel spirit is a life of chaos, confusion, and instability that ultimately leads to broken homes, marriages, relationships, churches, and utter destruction." Jezebel uses witchcraft to lead people astray and away from truth through deception and sin. She loves to use sexual perversions because that is what she is known for. She is a seducing spirit that will escort you right into immorality and idolatry. She uses the fleshly components of enticement, such as gossip, flattery, and false teachings and promises. Beware of her, and be sure you are not operating under this ungodly spirit.

"So I say, let the Holy Spirit guide your lives. Then you won't be doing what your sinful nature craves. The sinful nature wants to do evil, which is just the opposite of what the Spirit wants. And the Spirit gives us desires that are the opposite of what the sinful nature desires. These two forces are constantly fighting each other, so you are not free to carry out your good intentions. But when you are directed by the Spirit, you are not under obligation to the law of Moses." (Galatians 5:16-18, NLT)

Psychics and Mediums

For me growing up, looking up your current monthly horoscope was the fun thing to do. It tickled your ear and told you some amazing things that were supposedly going to occur and never did, but have you ever thought about the root of a thing? What god are they getting this information from because it certainly is not from Jesus Christ? "This is not the wisdom that comes down from above, but is earthly, unspiritual, and demonic." (James 3:15, ESV)

God's promises are Yes and Amen and do not come back unsettled. Who goes searching for darkness to be entered into your life anyway? Medium spirits provide a demonic fantasy illusion of life expectations and future events. They give out this false self delusion that they are releasing supernatural dreams and truths; when they are really releasing and escorting dark forces into your life. Witchcraft also is known as "the knowledge from below and the rejection of knowledge from above".

I had a co-worker years ago who flew cross country to see a psychic with her family to discuss their future. When she returned back to work, she was completely different. She had a false confidence that seemed so eerie. Things began to change in her life, and seemed as if she was excelling, but just a couple of years later, the temporary success was gone. Those spirits are tricky, manipulating, and will force you out of God's will for your life. Only one thing is for sure, and that is the promises of God (Jesus). Other false gods can't guarantee us anything but disaster. The bible warns in many verses of the destruction that comes from dabbling in this area.

❖ *"And the Lord said to me, 'The prophets are prophesying lies in my name. I did not send them, nor did I command them or speak to them. They are prophesying to you a lying vision, worthless divination, and the deceit of their own minds.'" (Jeremiah 14:14, ESV)*

❖ *"Someone may say to you, 'Let's ask the mediums and those who consult the spirits of the dead. With their whisperings and mutterings, they will tell us what to do.' But shouldn't people ask God for guidance? Should the living seek guidance from the dead?"(Isaiah 8:19-22, NLT)*

❖ *"Do not defile yourselves by turning to mediums or to those who consult the spirits of the dead. I am the Lord your God." (Leviticus 19:31, NLT)*

❖ *"I will also turn against those who commit spiritual prostitution by putting their trust in mediums or in those who consult the spirits of the dead. I will cut them off from the community. (Leviticus 20:6, NLT)*

❖ *"Men and women among you who act as mediums or who consult the spirits of the dead must be put to death by stoning. They are guilty of a capital offense." (Leviticus 20:27, NLT)*

❖ *"The light of a lamp will never shine in you again. The happy voices of brides and grooms will never be heard in you again. For your merchants were the greatest in the world, and you deceived the nations with your sorceries." (Revelation 18:23, NLT)*

❖ *"So Saul died because he was unfaithful to the Lord. He failed to obey the Lord's command, and he even consulted a medium instead of asking the Lord for guidance. So the Lord killed him and turned the kingdom over to David son of Jesse." (1 Chronicles 10:13, NLT)*

❖ *"Refusing to obey is as bad as the sin of sorcery. Being stubborn and doing what you want is like the sin of worshiping idols. You refused to obey the Lord's command, so He now refuses to accept you as king." (1 Samuel 15, ERV)*

❖ *"Manasseh also sacrificed his own sons in the fire in the valley of Ben-Hinnom. He practiced sorcery, divination, and witchcraft, and he consulted with mediums and psychics. He did much that was evil in the Lord's sight, arousing his anger." (2 Chronicles 33:6, NLT)*

Idols

"I am the Lord your God, who brought you out of the land of Egypt, out of the house of slavery. You shall have no other gods before me. You shall not make yourself a carved image, or any likeness of anything that is in heaven above, or that is in the earth beneath, or that is in the water under the earth. You shall not bow down to them or serve them, for I, the Lord your God, am a jealous God, visiting the iniquity of the fathers on the children to the third and the fourth generation of those who hate me." (Exodus 20:15, ESV)

When we think of worshipping idols, we often automatically think of statues or some type of foreign objects, but anything or anyone we put before God is considered an idol. These are things that take up God's place in our lives. It could be our careers, our relationships, money, and addictions, such as sexual perversions, drugs, alcoholism, Internet (social media), and even other people.

Whatever we do, we are to do it unto the Lord [for His glory] (1 Corinthians 10:31). What has your space? What is the first thing you do in the morning? Do you hit the floor on your knees and have a conversation with your Lord and Savior? Or do you grab your phone first? You have no business talking to anyone else before you have spoken to God first. Amen!

I remember reading on a social media site about "The church of Beyoncé" where fans gathered and participated in a worship service devoted to her. Somehow, they combine and intertwine her music, bible scripture, and a sermon together. Plain and simple, this was a ceremony of idol worship and more than likely some other none sense of demonic activity mixed in.

We are to keep ourselves protected with God's armor to prevent us from falling into this area of witchcraft. We have to guard our ears, eyes, hearts, and minds and renew them daily. Truth is you don't know who worshiped what in your bloodline or what they dabbled in or who they dabbled in it with. Repent to God for your ancestors and for any participation you may have had in witchcraft or idol worship. Leave no stone unturned. You can only get to heaven through Jesus Christ and not any other god.

- ❖ *"For the wages of sin is death; but the gift of God is eternal life through Jesus Christ our Lord." (Romans 6:23, KJV)*

- ❖ *"Put to death therefore what is earthly in you: sexual immorality, impurity, passion, evil desire, and covetousness, which is idolatry." (Colossians 3:5, ESV)*

Our King of Glory (Jesus)

❖ *"And I beheld, and I heard the voice of many angels round about the throne and the beasts and elders; and the number of them was ten thousand times ten thousand, and thousands of thousands; saying with a loud voice, Worthy is the Lamb that was slain to receive power, and riches, and wisdom, and strength, and honour, and glory, and blessing." (Revelation 5:11-12, KJV)*

How worthy is Jesus Christ to you? He is the most valuable thing to us because without Him, we are nothing. 1 Samuel 2:30 says that if we honor Him, He will release honor unto us. We must humble ourselves to the hand of God and give the glory and honor that is due to Him. Everything submits to the King of Glory. We were created and designed to worship and glorify Him; the man that died for you and me. All power is in His hands and He gave that same power to us because we have the glory of His inheritance. Psalms 8:5 says He has crowned us with glory and honor.

We operate in the power of God and we carry the same glory through our Lord and Savior Jesus Christ. So why worship something or someone who can't do anything for you. Our God is the only person who we can completely depend on. He is the one who meets our needs. He is the only one who forgives, who restores, who delivers, who heals, who strengthens, and who provides for us. Great is our Lord. He is our hope of glory according to Colossians 1:27 and releases riches unto to us.

Everything we need, especially to advance the kingdom, is given to us. What we give to Jesus, He gives it right back to us. Psalms 84:11 (KJV) says, "For the Lord God is a sun and shield; the Lord will give grace and glory: no good thing will He withhold from them that walk uprightly."

These riches are locked into Jesus and can only be released through Him and not anything or anyone else. Truth is, nobody is going to fight for you like our Lord and Savior will. He is the author and the finisher of our faith. If you have participated in idol worship, you must dismiss and renounce it out of your life in the Name of Jesus. We want the fullness of His blessings over our lives and not that of demonic curses by dabbling in things not of God. Whatever dishonor that you have proclaimed, reverse it, repent, and disassociate yourself with that thing or person.

❖ *"Christ hath redeemed us from the curse of the law, being made a curse for us...." (Galatians 3:13, KJV)*

All deceitfulness, craftiness, and wickedness regarding worshiping anything other than Christ Jesus, cast it out of your mind, your heart, and actions. Don't lift your life up to idols, for they can only make empty promises and leave you unsatisfied. Everything we do and everything in us, we submit it under the authority of Jesus Christ. You want clean hands and a pure heart. We are to be those that seek His face and His face ONLY. Jesus must be the Lord of your life; He is our King of Glory.

❖ *"Who is the king of glory? The Lord strong and mighty, the Lord might in battle." (Psalms 24:8, KJV)*

❖ *"Again, the devil took Him to a very high mountain and showed Him all the kingdoms of the world and their glory. And he said to Him, 'All these I will give you, if you will fall down and worship me.' Then Jesus said to him, 'Be gone, Satan! For it is written, "You shall worship the Lord your God, and Him only shall you serve."' (Matthew 4:8-10, ESV)*

❖ *"For I alone am God! I am God, and there is none like me." (Isaiah 46:9, NLT)*

❖ *"I do not want you to be participants with demons. You cannot drink the cup of the Lord and the cup of demons. You cannot partake of the table of the Lord and the table of demons. (1 Corinthians 10:20-21, ESV)*

❖ *"Their idols are silver and gold, the work of human hands. They have mouths, but do not speak: eyes, but do not see. They have ears, but do not hear; noses, but do not smell. They have hands, but do not feel; feet, but do not walk; and they do not make a sound in their throat. Those who make them become like them, so do all who trust in them. (Psalms 115:4-8, ESV)*

❖ *"But the hour is coming, and is now here, when the true worshipers will worship the Father in Spirit and truth, for the Father is seeking such people to worship Him." (John 4:23, ESV)*

❖ *"Do not turn to idols or make for yourselves any gods of cast metal: I am he Lord your God." (Leviticus 19:4, ESV)*

❖ *"For all the gods of the peoples are worthless idols, but the Lord made the heavens." (Psalms 96:5, ESV)*

❖ *"For rebellion is as the sin of divinations [witchcraft], and presumption is as iniquity and idolatry. Because you have rejected the word of the Lord, He has also rejected you from being king." (1 Samuel 15:23, ESV)*

Declaration Prayer

Lord, I repent of witchcraft and idol worship in my life and within my bloodline. I cancel and rebuke any idols and powers of darkness in any area of my life, and I proclaim the only Name that is above all names, my Lord and Savior Jesus Christ who rests, rules, and abides in my heart, mind, and soul. I pray that your all-consuming fire burns away any idols and any spirits that try to exalt it-self above you Lord. You are the master of my life and everything around me. I will carry your glory to the ends of the earth and will serve you for the rest of my days. My future generations will serve the one true King, Jesus Christ, and we will submit to your author-ity and no other name will we call upon. You are our master and savior. Any generational false god or idol present in my bloodline must flee by the power of Jesus the one I serve. I renounce any connection and announce the name of the Lord as our Strong Tower in Jesus' Name.

CHAPTER 13

Generational Sexual Sins

❖ *"Now the works of the flesh are evident: sexual immorality, impurity, sensuality, idolatry, sorcery, enmity, strife, jealousy, fits of anger, rivalries, dissensions, divisions, envy, drunkenness, orgies, and things like these. I warn you, as I warned you before, that those who do such things will not inherit the kingdom of God". (Galatians 5:19-21, ESV)*

Perversion

It's not by chance that sexual sin is mentioned first in this scripture. It's also listed first in 1 Corinthians 6:9-11 "Or do you not know that the unrighteous will not inherit the kingdom of God? Do not be deceived: neither the sexually immoral, nor idolaters, no adulterers, nor men who practice homosexuality, or thieves, nor the greedy, nor drunkards, nor revilers, nor swindlers will inherit the kingdom of God…" This is obviously an important area that God wants us to defeat immediately.

1 Thessalonians 4 says that God wants us to be holy and that we should not let sexual desires control us like the people who do not know God. Perversion is the author of all sexual sins. It's a work of the flesh. Left unchecked, perversion can streamline into the deepest crevices of a person. Perversion will have you doing things

you never imagined you would do, but because your flesh is at the time being fed, it's stronger and winning to take over your mind and spirit. Lust also has deep connections to perversion. Lust is defined as uncontrolled or illicit sexual desire or appetite. Lust is never that of love, and it never satisfies. It doesn't care how it eats just as long as it gets fed. It will feed off whatever is going to keep it alive and make it grow.

Perversion is unhealthy and unnatural. That is why you see humans that have relations with animals and people who commit rapes, molestations, and incest. Men and women of great influence, leaders, and even pastors have lost the battle. That perverse spirit has gotten the best of them, taken over, and won control. Like lust, perversion is an unquenchable desire whose needs can never be met. The spirit of perversion is how people become addicted to pornography and who are involved in incest with family members. King David's son Amnon had a spirit of lust and perversion. He raped his own sister Tamar in 2 Samuel 13.

It's the spirit of perversion that causes us to fall into sexual sin, to commit adultery, to fornicate, to be with others of the same sex, or to fantasize about being with them. Pornography seems to be one of the most popular areas of perversion. The bible isn't telling us to guard our ear and eye gates for nothing. It's to keep us focused on the things of God. We can't let our bodies be over taken by lustful thinking and actions. Luke 11:34 (ESV) says, "Your eye is the lamp of your body. When your eye is healthy, your whole body is filled of light, but when it is bad, your body is filled of darkness." Once you start participating in these sins, they become harder to break and defeat. Perversion is a never ending cycle that passes down through the generations. Even if there's been no evidence of the spirit of perversion within your family, you need to still stay aware. Maintain your stance and your purity. Know your triggers. What triggers your urges and makes you act on them? Is it rejection or abandonment? Find the root of this spirit and be free.

Declaration Prayer

Thank you Father for cleansing me of all unrighteousness. For my body is not my own, but it is yours Lord. I command and decree that anything unlike you be removed from my bloodline in The Name of Jesus Christ. Search me and my blood. Forgive us Father of our sins. Remove any memories of sexual sin from my mind, body, and soul. I am clean and I am whole. No perverse spirit will overtake me. I win because I keep my mind on the things of God and turn from wickedness and all seducing spirits. My eye gates are clean. My ear gates are clean. I am free and delivered from the spirit of perversion in The Name of Jesus.

Unequally yoked

❖ *"Do not be unequally yoked with unbelievers. For what partnership has righteousness with lawlessness? Or what fellowship has light with darkness?" (2 Corinthians 6:14, ESV)*

Selfish desires play a major role in being in an unequally yoked relationship or marriage. Some may think, "I'm 45, I'll never find anyone else, this is the best I'm going to get." So you settle. Or some may say, "He's not that bad, I can change him to love God and go to church". Marriage is already a huge responsibility and takes a lot of work. Do you really want that extra load to try to force someone to change? What if they never do what you thought they would? Then, you're stuck being miserable or going to divorce court because you're expecting more out of someone than they actually want to give you. When you force things to go in certain directions out of selfish desires, you're not being obedient to the perfect will of our Father.

You thought you were fighting against a simple soul tie, but you had sexual relations with a person or even married a person who was an atheist or of a different faith and believed in other occult things. You later realized you're fighting another realm of demonic forces. You are now unequally bound with a force that is working overtime to overtake your relationship with the one true living God (Jesus). You've just entered yourself into ungodly agreements and covenants.

Ask questions and know what you are entering into. Before you marry, find out details. Because whatever is going on in the family, when you marry, you are inheriting the family issues. This is why premarital counseling is so important. Be humble, get advice, and have some wisdom poured into you. During counseling, possible problems can be identified and the work to find resolve can begin. Know who you are marrying. Don't go into covenant with families just as messed up as yours. You better ask a thousand questions and observe for yourself. Your future and sanity depend on it.

Declaration Prayer

Lord, equip with wisdom and discernment to see who I should be connected with in life. Forgive me Lord and help me disconnect from all ungodly and unhealthy relationships; whether at work, ministry, or my personal life. Only connect me with God ordained relationships. The people that you place in my life, we are equally yoked and declare Jesus as our Lord and Savior. We are on the same page and our hearts gravitate towards you. I will not compromise and bind myself into any covenant agreements non-believers. I trust you and put my relationships into your hands in Jesus' Name Amen!

Soul ties

When we understand that the devil wants our souls for keeps, that realization will change our perspective on what we allow to operate in our lives. He comes by all means necessary and will stop at nothing to get to you. He wants to kill you, steal from you, and destroy any good part of any good thing associated with you. That's why he makes ungodly soul ties so easily available for us to get involved in.

Have you ever been involved with someone you knew was sent by the devil, but because you wanted to feel good at the moment, you caved in to the temptation of sexual sin? Ungodly soul ties are when you tie your soul to the wrong person. Soul ties occur when some of the other person's soul is intertwined and mingling with your soul. His addictions are now your addictions. His lusts and perversions are now your lusts and perversions. Things that you have never struggled with before, you now struggle with. You now have your problems mixed in with a host of everyone else' problems that you have been intimate with. Have you ever wondered why you do the things that you really don't want to do? Be careful to whom you give your body or whose body you have been in because it can cause you to carry some unwanted loads.

With soul ties, you are not just giving your body or entering into another body, you are creating a covenant. Covenants are for marriage and with Jesus. The greatest covenant of all times is the blood covenant you have with our Lord and Savior Jesus Christ.

His blood is the only blood you want running through your veins, but our selfish ambitions and actions get in the way of us doing what's right.

When soul ties attach themselves to you, they don't want to let you go, and it will seem almost impossible to untangle yourself from them. You can become addicted to people even when you don't really want or like them. You will find yourself going back even after you said I will never sleep with him again. It's so hard to break away from a soultie. It's the sin in us that causes us to make bad choices and decisions. "I don't understand why I act the way I do. I don't do the good I want to do, and I do the evil I hate. And if I don't want to do what I do, that means I agree that the law is good. But I am not really the one doing the evil. It is sin living in me that does it." (Romans 7:15-17, ERV).

Sexual sins become an addictive habit that you can't kick. You know it's bad for you, but you just can't seem to put it down and just stop cold turkey. Soul ties can make you look crazy, foolish, and petty. I've rode past houses late at night; I've blocked my number only to call and hang up after they answered; I've stalked social media accounts, and I've thought of them obsessively. It's a struggle to overcome a soul tie, and even if you think you are over the person, unless you have completely cleansed that spirit out of you by true repentance, discipline, and obedience, it's still in you.

It's an emotional attachment. You will still walk around with it, go home to it, eat with it, sleep with it, and even go to church with it. Years have gone by, and now you've passed these struggles of perversion down to your children who never asked for any of those problems. Things from someone you probably barely knew has now affected and infected your bloodstream for generations until someone decides to stand up and fight for the cleansing to be completed. Is that person you? Will you stand and fight because the obstacle is bigger than you think it is.

You thought you were clear from sexually transmitted diseases, but did you know that you can get spiritual STDs from people? Spiritually transmitted diseases (STDs) have long range effects just as a physical STD, and in some cases they are much worse. You don't know what people have got or what they are dealing with and now you're picking up habits that you've seen in them.

All of a sudden, your mind is thinking wrong thoughts that are all messed and mixed up. You're hanging with bad company and people you would normally not hang around. Your symptoms become the same as theirs, and now you have caught what they have: anger, thoughts of suicide, mixed emotions, depression, bad attitudes, and much more.

We must get rid of the spirits that are lurking and lying dormant. Because all it will take is one interference, one interception, or for them to truly come up and out in full force. You may say, "Well, I've never struggled with that before, so I'm good". No, you're not. If this perverse spirit runs in your family, you'd better be on watch, alert and know what's going on inside of you so you can get the right spiritual meds to begin your healing.

Declaration Prayer

Lord, forgive me, save me, and deliver me from ungodly soul ties. Rip and break the unwanted connection with _____ and free me from the attachment of their soul. Free me from any spirits not like you that I allowed to enter through sexual sin. Disconnect me from all ungodly soul ties. The demonic chain connections are broken in my life in the Name of Jesus. I am FREE! I will seek you first and will wait and prepare for my spouse. My body is yours Lord AMEN.

Fornication

❖ *"The Lord sees everything, and He watches us closely. Sinners are trapped and caught by their own evil deeds. They get lost and die because of their foolishness and lack of self-control." (Proverbs 15:21-23, CEV)*

Plain and simple, fornication is sex outside of marriage. It is unlawful sexual intercourse, including adultery. It seems that in today's society, fornication is the norm; okay to do, and is highly accepted and in some instances, it's even recommended. People live with the opposite sex before marriage because they want to "test the waters" before making a life decision. Well, I've been there and done that and let me tell you that anything that is not built with Jesus at the center will fall, so it's pointless and devastating to even try or think it will all work out. It's an out of order commitment; and that commitment sometimes brings forth children out of wedlock as a result.

The bible clearly says to "flee fornication" in 1 Corinthians 6:18 (KJV). Then it goes on to say that if you commit sexual sin, you are sinning against your own body. We should know that our bodies are a temple of the Holy Spirit that we received from God and that lives in us. We do not own ourselves. Fornication is a trap of the enemy that develops soulties and entices us to move on to commit adultery and other sexual sins. God paid a very high price to make us free from strongholds, lusts and perversions, so we should honor God with our bodies.

Self pleasuring is also a sexual sin. Masturbation may seem innocent to some, but it can cause just as much inner damage as other sexual sins. As a single person, you won't die if you live without sex. It's not a need, but a desire that was initially created for marriage only. You don't need sex; you need self control to resist the temptations. You need self control over your thoughts and the fantasying that comes along with masturbating. It pulls and takes something from you; plus adds unwanted weights and demonic activity inside each time you enter into that area. I once heard an evangelist say that when you masturbate, you are having sex with demons. This blew my mind, but I understood. You wonder why you have suddenly started self pleasuring yourself when you've never had the desire before? Think back to those ungodly soul ties you formed with people from your past. You thought you were threw with them, but they may still be dreaming and fantasying about you while masturbating; and sending those spirits your way. This spirit is deeper than you think, but you can be free by the power of Jesus Christ. Pray against anyone doing masturbation towards you and come against the enemy of any sort of sexual sin.

❖ *"Abstain from all appearance of evil. And the very God of peace sanctify you wholly; and I pray God your whole spirit and soul and body be preserved blameless unto the coming of our Lord Jesus Christ." (1 Thessalonians 5:22-23, KJV)*

❖ *"Let marriage be held in honor among all, and let the marriage bed be undefiled, for God will judge the sexually immoral and adulterous." (Hebrews 13:4, ESV)*

❖ *"But as for the cowardly, the faithless, the detestable, as for murders, the sexually immoral, sorcerers, idolaters, and all liars, their portion will be in the lake that burns with fire and sulfur, which is the second death." (Revelation 21:8, ESV)*

❖ *"Food is meant for the stomach and the stomach for food—and God will destroy both one and the other. The body is not meant for sexual immorality, but for the Lord, and the Lord for the body." (1 Corinthians 6:13, ESV)*

❖ *"But sexual immorality and all impurity or covetousness must not even be named among you, as is proper among saints." (Ephesians 5:3, ESV)*

❖ *"If we confess our sins, he is faithful and just to forgive us our sins and to cleanse us from all unrighteousness." (1 John 1:9, ESV)*

❖ *"I appeal to you therefore, brothers, by the mercies of God, to present your bodies as a living sacrifice, holy and acceptable to God, which is your spiritual worship…" (Romans 12:1, ESV)*

❖ *"If they cannot exercise self-control, they should marry. For it is better to marry than to burn with passion." (1 Corinthians 7:9, ESV)*

Declaration Prayer

Father, I bring any sexual sin and perverse spirit that is in my life to the foot of the cross. I break and sever all ungodly soulties with former sexual partners by the blood of Jesus. Lust must go! Perversion must go! Release and erase any sexual memories or emotions associated with former sexual partners. Cleanse my mind, my heart, and my temple. I submit my body to you. Lord, heighten my awareness of sin so that when I am tempted, I will be strong and I will not fall. Convict my spirit that I will always turn from evil. I resist the devil, and he flees from me. I am holy and walk in sexual purity in the Name of Jesus.

Adultery

❖ *"Now, about sex and marriage; Drink only the water that comes from your own well, and don't let your water flow out into the streets. Keep it for yourself and don't share it with strangers. Be happy with your own wife. Enjoy the woman you married while you were young. She is like a beautiful deer, a lovely fawn. Let her love satisfy you completely. Stay drunk on her love and don't go stumbling into the arms of another woman." (Proverbs 5:15-20, ERV)*

The spirit of fornication gives birth to adultery, whether physically or mentally. Believe it or not, you can commit adultery without actually cheating physically on your spouse. This type of adultery occurs when you give someone else your emotional attention or when you fantasize about another married person in a way that is sexual. You have still committed adultery. You may say, "Well, he and his wife are separated." You have still committed adultery. "Well, his wife lives in a different state, and they have been separated for three years." You have still committed adultery. Don't cross that bridge if they have not signed on the dotted line. Scripture says, "You know the commandment which says, 'Be faithful in marriage.' But I tell you if you look at another woman and want her, you are already unfaithful in your thoughts." (Matthew 5:27-28 CEV).

You just don't slip into the sin of adultery and fornication; it was planned. You planned to go to his house. You invited her over. You bought the cute lingerie. You answered the call at midnight. It was all premeditated.

I've fallen into adultery unknowingly and knowingly. Not knowing that guys were married or buying into the whole "we are separated" lies. Even worse, knowing that the man was married, I still let my flesh completely take over my mind and my body. Either way, I played my part in the sin of adultery and it was wrong, but I'm so thankful to God for His blood that washes us clean.

The enemy's tricks aren't broad and general; they are customized specifically for you. He knows what you are attracted to and what triggers your urges; whether it is his looks, his body, his personality or others as such. I was single and had been celibate for years. I hadn't even dated or entertained the company of a man. I was focused on God and my ministry. The enemy knows who and what will make you fall; remember his plans are strategic. The enemy has no new tricks, so always keep your guard up; because the minute you let it down, the enemy will be waiting right there. He will fool you and make a fool out of you.

He brought a married man along that was familiar to me. I was comfortable around him and had known him for years. We both crossed boundaries that we should have never crossed and did things I never thought I would ever do. Adultery will always start off subtle with great laughs, things in common, then small spaces of alone time where no one else is around for accountability. This opens doors for the enemy to be bolder and take bigger steps. Then the next thing you know, you've jumped into the deep end of the pool and now you're drowning in the sexual sin of adultery. Don't do it! It will cause more pain than pleasure for both parties and their families.

Be sure to set keep your armor on and set your mind on the things above; whether single or married. The enemy does not care, he wants to destroy godly marriages and destroy your stance of purity and wholeness as a single person.

❖ *"But because of the temptation to sexual immorality, each man should have his own wife and each woman her own husband." (1 Corinthians 7:2, ESV)*

❖ *"You shall not commit adultery." (Exodus 20:14, ESV)*

❖ *"Let marriage be held in honor among all, and let the marriage bed be undefiled, for God will judge the sexually immoral and adulterous." (Hebrews 13:4, ESV)*

❖ *"I have seen your abominations, your adulteries and neighings, your lewd whorings, on the hills in the field. Woe to you, O Jerusalem! How long will it be before you are made clean?" (Jeremiah 13:27, ESV)*

❖ *"He who commits adultery lacks sense; he who does it destroys himself." (Proverbs 6:32, ESV)*

❖ *"You have heard that it was said, 'You shall not commit adultery.' But I say to you that everyone who looks at a woman with lustful intent has already committed adultery with her in his heart." (Matthew 5:27-28, ESV)*

❖ *"If we confess our sins, He is faithful and just to forgive us our sins and to cleanse us from all unrighteousness." (1 John 1:9, ESV)*

Declaration Prayer

Father, forgive me for breaking the vows of marriage. Cleanse me and my bloodline from the sin of adultery. Adultery and marriage-breaking spirits are destroyed in my life and in my bloodline. I will never go back and from this day forth, I will do what is right and run away from evil. I honor you with my body and my actions are pleasing in your sight. I am faithful in my marriage and my eyes are only set toward my spouse. I cast down adulterous imaginations in my mind and body. I bring into captivity every rebellious thought and replace it with the word of God. Whatever is true, honorable, just, pure, lovely, and commendable; I think on those things. I bind any seductive spirits that have plans or schemes to make me fall into the sin of adultery. Give me the power of the Holy Spirit to overcome every temptation. Break every soul tie that has been created with anyone other than my spouse. I thank you for a fresh love and fire for my spouse in Jesus' Name.

Homosexuality

❖ *"You shall not lie with a male as with a woman; it is an abomination." (Leviticus 18:22, ESV)*

The spirit of perversion causes you never to be satisfied. Not even satisfied with the way our Heavenly Father created us to be: man with woman. With homosexuals, we see women with women and men with men. There are men who want to become women, and women who want to become men. This is an identity crisis and is not godly. Our God doesn't make any mistakes. Every organ, every feature, and every detail He made with you specifically in mind. The enemy wants us to think differently and is good at lying and tricking us into not living out who God created us to be.

Homosexual behaviors violate God's intended plan for marriage and family. Marriage is to be between a man and a woman. Any sexual act outside of marriage is considered adultery whether it is heterosexual or homosexual contact. It's backwards thinking to believe that you can be satisfied by a same sex partner. It is not the way God intended marriage relationships to be and is considered unnatural. It's a spirit of perversion and an abomination unto the Lord. The word of God is very clear on this subject and there are no exceptions to according to His word.

Decree that your children will not inherited or struggle with the same perversions that once gripped you or members of your family. Repent of these sexual sins and be delivered from all unclean spirits In Jesus Name!

❖ *"For this reason God gave them up to dishonorable passions. For the women exchanged natural relations for those that are contrary to nature; and the men likewise gave up natural relations with women and were consumed with passion for one another, men committing shameless acts with men and receiving in themselves the due penalty for their error." (Romans 1:26-27, ESV)*

❖ *"So God created man in His own image, in the image of God He created him; male and female He created them." (Genesis 1:27, ESV)*

❖ *"Or do you not know that the unrighteous will not inherit the kingdom of God? Do not be deceived: neither the sexually immoral, nor idolaters, nor adulterers, nor men who practice homosexuality, nor thieves, nor greedy, nor drunkards, nor revilers, nor swindlers will inherit the kingdom of God." (1 Corinthians 6:9-10, ESV)*

❖ *"But from the beginning of creation, God made them male and female. Therefore, a man shall leave his father and mother and hold fast to his wife, and the two shall become one flesh. So they are no longer two but one flesh. What therefore God has joined together, let not man separate." (Mark 10:6-9, ESV)*

❖ *"If a man lies with a male as with a woman, both of them have committed an abomination; they shall surely be put to death; their blood is upon them." (Leviticus 20:13, ESV)*

❖ *"And such were some of you. But you were washed, you were sanctified, you were justified in the name of the Lord Jesus Christ and by the Spirit of God." (1 Corinthians 6:11, ESV)*

❖ *"Just as Sodom and Gomorrah and the surrounding cities, which likewise indulged in sexual immorality and pursued unnatural desire,*

serve as an example by undergoing a punishment of eternal fire."
(Jude 1:7, ESV)

❖ *"The law is not laid down for the just but for the lawless and disobedient, for the ungodly and sinners, for the unholy and profane, for those
who strike their fathers and mothers, for murders, for the sexually
immoral, men who practice homosexuality, enslavers, liars, perjurers,
and whatever else is contrary to sound doctrine…" (1 Timothy 1:8-
10, ESV)*

Declaration Prayer

Lord, forgive me of any homosexual behaviors and actions that I
have committed. Cleanse my bloodline and place things back into
your originally intended order. Refresh and renew my mind from
unclean spirits of perversions and lusts. I believe that you have
plans for me. I am satisfied in You. I am happy in You. No longer
am I confused about who I am. I know who I am in Christ Jesus. I
see clear and know that I am a child of God. I disconnect and turn
from my wicked ways and anyone connected to me that has a homosexual lifestyle. Spirits of confusion and homosexuality MUST
GO NOW in Jesus' Name! I am FREE!

The Ending of a Curse

Sin and routine patterns sometime lay dormant until something
awakens them to get up and start some action. These are demons
that need to be dealt with. If you are not sure what curse may lie
within your family, pray and ask God to bring the name of the
generational spirit to you so that you can rebuke, renounce, and
repent of the sin. We can't allow these curses and patterns to continue in our lives. We must choose who we will serve faithfully and

consistently. The Bible says to choose this day whom you will serve (Joshua 24:15). Either you will be in agreement with God's word, or you won't. Choose God and learn how to demagnetize yourself from curses that plague your family.

❖ *"Now therefore fear the Lord and serve him in sincerity and in faithfulness. Put away the gods that your fathers served beyond the River and in Egypt, and serve the Lord. And if it is evil in your eyes to serve the Lord, choose this day whom you will serve, whether the gods your fathers served in the region beyond the River, or the gods of the Amorites in whose land you dwell. But as for me and my house, we will serve the Lord." (Joshua 24:14-15, ESV)*

Declaration Prayer

We DECREE old demonic cycles are being replaced with new cycles of goodness and wholeness. Every demonic structure that has been formed has to break and flee. Lord, you fight on our behalf in the courtroom and close every portal of the enemy where he has no legal access into our lives. Restore everything that has been lost or stolen from our bloodline. We declare nothing missing and nothing broken in the Name of Jesus.

Now that we have exposed the enemy's tactics and recognize how they have operated within our family history, it is time to release these battles and curses back to the pits of hell where they came from. During the next couple of chapter teachings, one by one, we will begin to receive victories, see chains falling off, and receive breakthroughs after breakthroughs, SELAH!!

SECTION 3:

THE BREAK

CHAPTER 14

Cleansing Your Bloodline

❖ *"But if a wicked person turns away from all his sins that he has committed and keeps all my statues and does what is just and right, he shall surely live; he shall not die. None of the transgressions that he has committed shall be remembered against him; for the righteousness that he has done he shall live. Have I any pleasure in the death of the wicked, declares the Lord God, and not rather that he should turn from his way and live?" (Ezekiel 18:21-23, ESV)*

Repentance

One of the weapons to activate cleansing is repentance. Repentance is the action of repenting, sincere regret or remorse. When you repent, you are signifying that you will completely turn from evil doing and do good as it is according to the word of God. You are relaying that you are sorry for the sin that was committed and are requesting forgiveness and help to overcome. We are to repent daily for our sins that are known and unknown because sometimes we sin when we don't realize we are.

Ezekiel warned God's people to repent in chapter 33:11 (ERV) "You must say to them, The Lord God says: By my life, I swear that I don't enjoy seeing people die—not even evil people! I don't want them to die. I want them to come back to me. I want them to change their lives so that they can really live. So come back to me! Stop doing bad things! Why must you die, family of Israel?"

❖ *Isaiah 1:16-17 (NLT) says "Wash yourselves and be clean! Get your sins out of my sight. Give up your evil ways."*

Repent for the sins of your ancestors and then cease the old life of sin that you are in. This step calls for us to reach all the way back and repent for the sins, words, and actions that past generations have committed and also the sins that we have committed. Even if you do not know exactly what your past generations may have dealt with, ask for those things to be revealed. Begin the process of cleansing your bloodline so that you can move forward to break away from generational curses. Stop them once and for all and do not give the enemy legal right in continuing to poison and taint your bloodline because if you do not break the patterns and plateaus in your life, they will do everything in their power to break you. Repent, Renounce, and Rebuke everything not like God!

❖ *"Repent therefore, and turn back, that your sins may be blotted out."* *(Acts 3:19, ESV)*

❖ *"Whoever conceals his transgressions will not prosper, but he who confesses and forsakes them will obtain mercy." (Proverbs 28:13, ESV)*

❖ *"Bear fruit in keeping with repentance." (Matthew 3:8, ESV)*

❖ *"No, I tell you; but unless you repent, you will all likewise perish."* *(Luke 13:3, ESV)*

❖ *"I have not come to call the righteous but sinners to repentance."* *(Luke 5:32, ESV)*

❖ *"If we confess our sins, He is faithful and just to forgive us our sins and to cleanse us from all unrighteousness." 1 John 1:9, ESV)*

❖ *"Those whom I love, I reprove and discipline, so be zealous and repent." (Revelation 3:19, ESV)*

❖ *"Repent, for the kingdom of heaven is at hand." (Matthew 3:2, ESV)*

Prayer, Fasting, and Consecration

Be the change you want to see in your life and in the lives of others around you. Let's break these cycles and curses that have been set in place in your bloodline. You want the bad in your life to be cancelled out and for the good to be recycled back to you and yours. Those gifts, the talents, anointings, and witty inventions that your ancestors had…you want those things back and for them to remain permanently. Get those gifts flowing in your bloodline. Pray for special traits and abilities that you've never had before and watch God pour them into you as you learn to activate the blessings in your bloodline.

The change first starts in you. You are the initiator to drop these loads you have been carrying; loads that you need to drop at the altar and never look back. Take them there and leave them there to starve and die off of you. What aggravates spirits you are trying to get rid of? Starvation!!! Starve the flesh. Don't feed it ANYTHING. Crucify the flesh and break the enemy in half. Silence your flesh and get in His presence. Take those bad things that need to die into prayer. Reset you mind and your thinking and set new habits of success. Choose faith over flesh. God will revive you with a sound mind and clear thoughts; and then He will give you strategy, wisdom, and deliverance. Connect with the Father through prayer, fasting, and consecration continuously. What may have started in your family, will end, stop and finish in you. Break the dysfunction because IT IS FINISHED.

Prayer

❖ *"And the prayer of faith will save the one who is sick, and the Lord will raise him up. And if he has committed sins, he will be forgiven."* (James 5:15, ESV)

Prayer is the perfect opportunity to spend time and commune with God. It is mentioned over 250 times in the bible; the results are proven and benefits are endless. Prayer enables us to express our honor and praises to our God and to share and confess to Him every single bit of our heart. Prayer is an act of worship, discipline, and obedience. It signifies that we depend on Him in regard to every area of our lives; to lead us, guide us, equip us, provide for us and strengthen us. Prayer is in our best interest and is extremely valuable.

"Prayer is the supernatural vehicle that transports us back and forth between the natural and supernatural realms in order to extract God's plans for our lives and make them into earthly realities." (Suzette T. Caldwell)

Prayer is our job, our position, our responsibility, and our connection to our Heavenly Father. Prayer is powerful and is necessary, as we all need it to survive. It should be as common to us as the air we breathe. Prayer becomes life to our spirits as it connects us with our Lord and Savior. It shouldn't ever be considered an option, for it is actually our legal right to use. Myles Monroe once said that we are the most powerful creatures on this earth as humans. That's because we have power and authority to command things to happen and line up in order. Prayers give God permission to work on our behalf. Prayers enable change. God needs us to bring change on this earth. When prayers stop, God is unable to move. "Prayer is giving God permission to interfere in earth's affairs" (Myles Monroe). Faith without works is dead (James 2:26).

❖ *"Ask and it will be given to you; seek and you will find; knock and the door will be opened to you." (Matthew 7:7, ESV)*

❖ *"I tell you, you can pray for anything, and if you believe that you've receive it, it will be yours." (Mark 11:24, NLT)*

Prayers are commands that activate God to move on our behalf. If we aren't praying, then how can we expect change? Oh, but when we do pray, we can move mountains. Things start moving, atmospheres and circumstances start shifting, miracles, signs and wonders take place, and healing comes Prayers bring deliverance and anything we are lacking. Prayer results in us becoming agents of change. We have the power to command ourselves to live and not die, and our circumstances can work for our good because we love the Lord. The word of God says to us, "Don't worry about anything; instead, pray about everything. Tell God what you need, and thank Him for all He has done. Then you will experience God's peace, which exceeds anything we can understand. His peace will guard your hearts and minds as you live in Christ Jesus. (Philippians 4:6, NLT).

John Wesley said, "It seems that without God, man CANNOT and without man, God WILL NOT." Those words tell me that He wants us to ask of Him what we need, and when we draw close to God, he draws close to us. When we seek after Him with all our heart and believe by faith, God truly will answer our prayers. We think we are waiting on God to move in our lives and bring change, but really God is waiting on us to bring our petitions to Him. We are waiting on Him to touch us, but He is waiting on us to touch HIM.

Believe that the prayers that we pray are working for our good. Even when we do not see them coming into fruition quickly, we should rest assured that they are being handled behind the scenes in the spirit realm. God resurrects what He wants to live in you during your prayer time. The prayers we pray will never die, but live on in the lives of the people we have lifted in prayer. Some of the prayers that your great-great-great grandmother prayed over you decades ago are still activated and are in operation right now as we speak. They have never died. These types of prayers are considered generational blessings.

These blessings just don't come about instantly; someone positioned the blessing to come your way. Someone was on his or her knees and sowed the seed of prayer for you. Prayers must be activated, and it's our responsibility to make that happen. Activate your blessings; activate your healing and deliverance. Bring those things that you are believing God for to come to pass in your life! You have the power and authority to do so. Prayer is our legal right.

Pray Big and Receive Big! Nothing is too hard for God. It may seem like that loved one will never get delivered or saved. It may seem like the cancer that has been taking out several of your family members is never going to stop. Listen, It Can and It Will. You must believe. Strengthen your faith and declare change and movement to take place in your situation and family. "I tell you the truth, if you have faith even as small as a mustard seed, you can say to this mountain, move from here to there and it will move; Nothing will be impossible for you." (Matthew 17:20, NLT).

Fasting and Consecration

When you combine prayer with fasting and consecration, there are unlimited possibilities of what our God can do in your life. You are separating yourself from things that are unclean and not of

God. Just as prayer, fasting and consecration is not a choice, but a command. Matthew 6:16:18 (ESV) "Jesus says "When you fast…" He did not say if you fast, but when you fast. "When you fast, do not look gloomy like the hypocrites, for they disfigure their faces that their fasting may be seen by others. Truly, I say to you, they have received their reward. But when you fast, anoint your head and wash your face, that your fasting may not be seen by others but by your Father who is in secret. And your Father who sees in secret will reward you."

Fasting is a need for something greater from God. It's a sacrificial offering to give up something you love dearly. It's a consecrated time alone with the Father to gain new perspectives and to hear from only Him more distinctly. It builds our reliance upon our God in Heaven. We focus our attention on Him, and He does the same for us as always. Our eyes are fixed on Him which enables our hearts to beat in alignment together.

Pray and fast when you need to make important decisions and need answers that only the Father can bring. Pray and fast in times of desperation and turmoil. In fact, just pray and fast. No other resource will ever do. Prayer and fasting is your answer; it is your one and only source. There is no other option. Jesus says, "I am the way, and the truth, and the life. No one comes to the Father except through me." (John 14:6, ESV).

Set a consecrated time that is just His; only you and God. You must make time to be alone with Him continuously. Let it become a part of your daily life. The devil hates this part of your life because you're bringing about a sacrificial offering of yourself. New cycles of discipline are being created during this period. You're telling the enemy that you aren't weak, but stronger than any force sent against you. You are telling the enemy that your mind is clear, that your heart is focused on the Most High, and that you are open to receive what the Father has for you. You don't have time to waste with the enemy's ploys. Get positioned and get down and dirty to block the enemy's schemes with your mouth and PRAY.

Because we are in Jesus' bloodline, we should be praying and decreeing full restoration back to our bloodlines and that they are functioning the way our Lord created them to function. Reverse and restore everything that has been tainted or lost. Reverse bad blood and close the portals that were once open so that the enemy does not have any legal way or right back into your life.

One thing to remember is to be persistent and consistent in prayer. Jesus told a parable regarding praying always and never loosing heart (Luke 18:1). The bible says never to let the word of God depart from your mouth (Joshua 1:8). This tells me that I am to pray without ceasing (1 Thessalonians 5:17). Jesus was a prayer warrior, and he learned from the best. "The Son...can do only what He sees his Father doing" (John 5:19). If Jesus did it, then we are to as well. Pray at all times and in everything always.

Hindered Prayers

Our prayers are sometimes hindered, and we don't know why, but once we let God in and allow Him to guide us to an examination of our hearts and circumstances, we can be get back in alignment with Him, and then we can receive freedom and deliverance from whatever has a hold on us. It all goes back to receiving revelation of knowledge as discussed in Chapter 1.

1 Peter 3:7 (NLT) gives an example of what could hinder your prayers. "In the same way, you husbands must give honor to your wives. Treat your wife with understanding as you live together. She

may be weaker than you are, but she is your equal partner in God's gift of new life. Treat her as you should so your prayers will not be hindered."

For this very reason, it's important for us to know how to pray, what to pray for, what to ask for, and what exact words to say that will bring to pass what we are requesting. Most importantly, we should pray and ask God to remove any blockages that are hindering us from receiving answered prayers and blessings.

Jesus teaches us this through his word. The disciples asked Jesus:

"Lord, teach us to pray, just as John taught his disciples. He said to them, 'When you pray, say: Our Father which art in heaven, Hallowed be thy name. Thy kingdom come. Thy will be done, as in heaven, so in earth. Give us day by our daily bread. And forgive us our sins; for we also forgive everyone that is indebted to us. And lead us not into temptation, but deliver us from evil.'" (Luke 11:1, KJV)

Another way to make your prayers most effective is to pray the scriptures. You can't go wrong using this method. God's word will accomplish exactly what it was sent out to do and will not come back void. "So shall my word be that goeth forth out of my mouth: it shall not return unto me void, but it shall accomplish that which I please, and it shall prosper in the thing whereto I sent it." (Isaiah 55:11, KJV).

Read and memorize the word of God. When we meditate on it, it gets into our hearts and changes us forever. The word does a complete makeover from the inside out in our lives. It's a never changing guide, and it works. There's power and everything we need is in His word. It's sharper than any two-edged sword; it cannot be destroyed, and it finishes what it starts.

Keep It Going

Don't give up on your prayers. Keep praying and keep believing. Keep recycling those prayers until you see the new cycles forming. Your faith will produce your outcome. The woman with the issue of blood had faith (Luke 8:43-48). She pressed through the crowd and believed by faith that all she had to do was touch the hem of Jesus' garment and she would be made well. If she would have given up, she would have never received her miracle. She put her faith into action and her faith healed her. Faith without works is dead (James 2:26).

Keep the endurance and let the scriptures be your influence and encouragement. It may seem foolish to some to believe and ask for mega things, but mega things are going to take mega prayers. I personally love it when the unexpected happens, and things are beyond my control. It forces me to trust in my God who is my helper and waymaker. It allows me to cast my cares and burdens upon Him. He takes it and fixes it; maybe not always as I planned, but it always ends up being what is best for me.

That's why I love my Abba Father. He cares and is concerned with the things that concern us. He enjoys it when we bring our petitions to Him. He hears them when we call on His name and guess what? He answers those prayers too. He cares about His greatest creations (His children) and wants to hear from us daily, so bring your petitions to Him.

Speak From Your Mouth (Decree and Declare)

❖ *...The God who gives life to the dead and speaks of things that don't yet exist as if they are real." (Romans 4:17, ERV)*

The tongue is a powerful member that enables us to speak, bless, declare, decree, command, move, shift and change atmospheres. It causes things to line up that were crooked and out of place or alignment. We can even command time reversal of our past by reversing and cancelling curses off of our lives. We can speak and declare that the things that the devil stole will come back to us 100 fold. We can reverse curses and cycles and speak life over ourselves. The tongue is a powerful part of the body.

We can also bring unwanted things upon ourselves by the words we speak. Do not let one word slip you back to where you used to be. There is power in what we say and what we say we have and will get. We will either agree with heaven or agree with hell. This is important to know in order for us not to settle with the things of the past and think since it has always been this way; it will always be that way. No, we have the power to speak and regain the time that we have lost.

Our God is outside of time and goes before us to fix the future and or the past. We have a God who will move heaven and earth on our behalf and nothing can stop Him from bringing His promises to the lives of His people. If He said it, it will be. He is the God who knows all and strengthens our faith so He can move on our behalf. There is no distance in His power and glory. He is right here for us watching and waiting every step of the way.

The bible tells us that Jesus prayed heaven open (Luke 3:21). When we declare, the heavens are opened and things will start pouring down upon our command. We have the power! Prayer stirs things up like a tornado and rolls out whirlwind blessings.

Pray bold and big prayers. Don't just believe God for an apartment, believe Him for a home. Speak it! Just don't pray that your child will get good grades, but that they will exceed expectations with straight A's, go to college, receive scholarships, and earn a salary above and beyond what you ever thought or imagined it could be. Speak it! His word says it. Just don't pray for your healing alone, speak that the sickness and disease is eliminated completely and will never touch your body or anyone else connected to you in the Name of Jesus.

Be sure to pray about everything. Speak everything good over your life! Don't leave anything uncovered or unturned because the devil does not want us digging deeper and finding revelation and knowledge. He wants us to stay naïve and non-alert to our surroundings and the forces of darkness.

Scripture also tells us that if we ask for anything in Jesus' my name, He will do it for you. Then the Father's glory will be shown through the Son (John 14:13-14). This scripture tells me that we should be praying about EVERYTHING and speaking the good in everything. One of my former pastors in Hinesville, GA, would always say that the words we speak out of our mouths have to attach themselves to something, whether good or bad. There's power in what we say; we will have what we say, so watch your mouth and what comes out of it.

Remember, nothing is too small or too big to take to our Father in Heaven. That's exactly what He wants from us: to make a sound, to open up our mouths and call on Him, to request and petition the needs and desires of our hearts, to tell Him what troubles us, and to request His guidance in unforeseen circumstances.

It doesn't matter what kind of past dirt you have. We have all been there, trust me! Some of us have been rolling around in dirt and mud for years. Even when the Israelites turned their backs on God, refused to obey, and refused to listen to the Lord's teaching, God's ear was still attentive to them. He still wanted to hear from them and show grace to them.

It says in Isaiah 30:18 (AMP), "Therefore, the Lord waits [expectantly] and longs to be gracious to you, And therefore He waits on high to have compassion on you. For the Lord is a God of justice; Blessed (happy, fortunate) are all those who long for Him [since He will never fail them]."

We need Him for everything in our lives. No one else can do the miraculous in our lives; only He can. He longs for us to know who He is and to have faith in His abilities as our Father. Open your mouth, boldly go before the throne of God, and make your petitions. Scripture says that we are not to be anxious about anything, but in every situation, by prayer and supplication with thanksgiving, let your requests be made known to God (Philippians 4:6).

When we open our mouths, we have the power to

- ♣ DECLARE – To be so, to speak into existence

- ♣ COMMAND – To instruct, to force, to order, to gain

- ♣ GRASP – To seize and hold firmly, to take possession,

- ♣ SECURE – To fix or attach something firmly so that it cannot be moved or lost

- ♣ PROMOTE – Advance or rise to a higher position or rank, to move up in elevation

- ♣ CHANGE – To replace, to make something different, to remove or to add.

- ♣ DISPELL – Eliminate, make disappear, banish

- ♣ REVERSE – To move, back off, cause to go the opposite way

- ♣ RENOUNCE – Abandon, refuse, reject

- ♣ DENOUNCE – Publicly declare to be wrong or evil, rail against, condemn

- ♣ REBUKE – Admonish, reprimand, scold, chastise

- ♣ CAST OUT – Let loose, set free, deliver

- ♣ WAR – Warfare, fight, attack

Speak and cancel out those agreements, contracts, and ungodly covenants in the Name of Jesus! Reverse the bad and add on the good. Speak, "I am a champion, I will speak victory and not defeat!" Speak who you are and who you want to be. "I am a kingdom builder and investor. I will build and invest in future generations. I am a God-made millionaire and my family is walking in wealthy places." Speak it into existence. Command your day, your morning, and your life to line up according to the word of God. Command future generations to come into order. Your children's children need your prophetic words right NOW!

After praying in the spirit throughout one day, God revealed to me that specific strongholds in my life had been broken and that neither the devil nor his demons had any access or legal right to me anymore. It was like all they could do was look at me and my loved ones through a window, but they could not touch me any further. Even regarding my job, God was telling me that the things I was worried about would be alright, and everything was going to work for my good because I diligently sought Him and had found favor in His sight. The weapons will not prosper.

One thing you need to remember is that God has got our backs because we are His kids. We are the King's Kids! His word does not come back void, but will accomplish and attach itself to every single thing it was sent out to do. Everything we speak, everything we command, everything we declare is OURS and will attach to what we say. I thank God for His power of our tongues (our heavenly language and weapons of mass destruction that will tear something up in the spirit realm). Use your prophetic voice. Speak what you don't see until you see it.

Put Your Assigned Angels to Work

God positioned assigned angels to work on our behalf. What are you waiting? They move on our command? They stand at attention waiting for you to open up your mouth and command the word of God over your day, your family, your job, your ministry, and your life. They are waiting on that sound that will open heaven. In the book of Daniel 10:12 (ESV), an angel went to Daniel and said, "Fear not, Daniel, for from the first day that you set your heart to understand and humbled yourself before your God, your words have been heard, and I have come because of your words."

They are here on earth to answer our prayers. Why not utilize these free resources? The line should be long and wrapped around the corner for some free stuff. They're giving away blessings, protection, and so much more! Reach up and grab them. It's an open heaven.

Why do we beg for things that we already have? Let the word work for you. Let the word do the work. That is exactly why you should be praying the scriptures. If you only knew what you are capable of changing around you with just the smack of your lips and tongue coming into agreement. If you only knew or could get a glimpse of how much damage you could do to the devil and his little imps and minions. If you only knew the full extent of what angels were created to do.

They were created to do God's will. To put it another way, there were created to be God's instruments or agents to carry out His work. In fact, the word "angel" actually means "messenger" or "agent". The Bible says, "Bless the Lord, O you His angels, you are mighty ones who do His word!" (Psalm 103:20, ESV).

They are on assignment to bring the things of heaven into the earth. To even get a glimpse of the work they do behind the scenes to guide us, protect us, cover us and prepare us would completely calm our spirits. They work overtime, and you have the nerve to say that you are tired. They are the answers we need, yet we don't even use them even though they are readily available.

- ♣ They fight strongholds and demonic forces on our behalf (Daniel 10:20; Revelation 12:7)

- ♣ They guide us (Mark 16:5-7; Acts 8:26

- ♣ They protect (Daniel 6:20-23; 2 Kings 6:13-17)

The angels will help and assist you in taking possession of your promises. Pray hard and strong. The harder and deeper you pray, the harder and deeper they will fight on your behalf. It's like having free legal services.

Display the Fruits of the Spirit

- ❖ *"But the fruit that the Spirit produces in a person's life is love, joy, peace, patience, kindness, goodness, faithfulness, gentleness, and self control." (Galatians 5:22, ERV)*

Displaying the fruit of the Spirit should be one of our main goals for our families. In order to produce that fruit, you have to be connected to the right root. If the root is problematic, then the fruit will be spoiled and not look or taste good. It will be bitter and molded from the inside out with dents and breaches all over it. Problems start at the root, work their way up on the inside, and then begin to manifest all that inside ugliness on the outside. Roots grow for years and become entangled and twisted, and for some, they have become sturdy weeds that are so deep that it seems they can't be pulled up. The difficulty in the weeds being pulled up is because they were formed from so many years and generations ago. They've had quite some time to grow deeper and develop a sturdy root.

It takes the right farmer…the right person…the right family member to understand the right strategy in knowing how to get that thing up out the ground and start fresh with some new soil. Jeremiah 4:3 tells us to plow our field and to not plant seeds among the fields of thorns. Think about the story of the farmer sowing the seed in the Bible (Mark 4). It says that the weeds grew and stopped the good plants from growing and did not make grain.

What fruit is your bloodline producing? Are they the fruit of the spirit? Do they mirror the image of our Father? No matter how strong the bad roots are in your life, I'm here to tell you that you are equipped and licensed to break up that fallow ground. If it's not life giving and honoring God, pull it up and take it out!

❖ *"Jesus said, 'I am the true vine, and my Father is the gardener. He cuts off every branch of mine that does not produce fruit. He also trims every branch that produces fruit to prepare it to produce even more. You have already been prepared to produce more fruit by the teaching I have given you. Stay joined to me and I will stay joined to you. No branch can produce fruit alone. It must stay connected to the vine. It is the same with you, You cannot produce fruit alone. You must stay joined to me.'" (John 15:2, ERV)*

❖ *"Sow to yourselves in righteousness, reap in mercy; break up your fallow ground: for it is time to seek the Lord, till He come and rain righteousness upon you." (Hosea 10:12, KJV)*

❖ *Cut demonic activity at the root and break off those evil habits and cycles. Clear the field, clear your mind, clear your heart, and start fresh. When we clear the mess out, then we will see and hear the Father more clearly. Stay open to HIM and receive the sweet fruit of the Spirit.*

❖ *"Oh, taste and see that the Lord is good! Blessed is the man who takes refuge in Him." (Psalm 34:8, ESV)*

Let your tree grow and produce that good fruit. Stay planted by your river; the living water that grows you, brings nutrients, and produces the fruit that you need. You never have to worry about anything if you keep God at the root, the center, the beginning, and the end of your life. AMEN!

CHAPTER 15

🔓

This Means WAR: It's time to FIGHT!

❖ *"The weapons we use are not human ones. Our weapons have power from God and can destroy the enemy's strong places. We destroy people's arguments, and we tear down every proud idea that raises itself against the knowledge of God. We also capture every thought and make it give up and obey Christ. We are ready to punish anyone there who does not obey, but first we want you to be fully obedient." (2 Corinthians 10:4, ERV)*

We no longer fight physically like in the bible days; now, we fight and war in the spirit. God has prepared us for war by training us for battle (Psalms 144:1). We have the ability and the strength to overcome and win whatever comes our way. John 14:12 tell us that if we believe in Him, we will do the same things He did. We will do greater works. So let's get to work. Don't accept the plans of the enemy. Don't lower your standards because you are too lazy to do the work. It will take a lot of work, but you have to make up in my mind that you are not playing with the enemy. Your life and the lives of others depend on it. Cut the enemy's head off (but before you do.... choke the life out of him). Sounds kind of violent huh? Well, he tried to do it to you!!!!

❖ *"From the days of John the Baptist until now the kingdom of heaven suffers violent assault, and violent men seize it by force [as a precious prize]." (Matthew 11:12, AMP)*

Let me tell you how serious this war is. Satan is trying to steal, kill, and destroy us and our families. He tried to take you and your children completely OUT. He put sickness on your mother. He came and shook up your marriage that resulted in divorce, he took over minds, you have kids in jail, and siblings on drugs. He even tried to ruin your reputation with lies. He needs to "GET GOT! Don't be simple minded when it comes to dealing with this joker. Key word is "joker" because he plays with people's minds, their insecurities, and their weaknesses until he finds a way in. The open portal which became his legal entry point as discussed earlier.

You have to pray and worship God like never before during this time. Opposition will come because you're on the right path and breaking walls downs. The enemy tries to disrupt only what is on course and productive. So you have to stand still when the attacks start coming toward you, knowing that you're fighting for greater good and you will win in the end. There may be times when it may look like a setback, but it is really a set up for the future. Keep fighting.

We know what we are up against. Now, you have to fight that devil up and out of you. Get smart and starve yourself of ungodly habits until it creates new, godly habits and cycles in your life. Remember, change starts with you. You must keep pushing even when you feel like things aren't changing fast enough. That's the devil talking because he knows you have almost broken through. You're almost to the finish line. Greater is right on the other side of the wall. Keep on praying and keep looking to God through the difficulties and stressful moments. Keep yourself moving forward and going up because the devil will send an army of people and circumstances to try to pull you back down. Reach out to God, just like the woman with the issue of blood.

Desperate times call for desperate measures. How bad do you want the change? Trust and believe that change is working behind the scenes and doing the things in the spirit realm that you and I cannot see. Trust that it's there and moving things on our behalf. Angels are helping us fight our battles. When it looks like hell has won, NO it has not. Our good is coming for us. Hold on and STAY IN THE FIGHT!

❖ *Psalms 84:11 (KJV) says, "No good thing will He withhold from them that walk uprightly". Hallelujah! Simply put, I'll be receiving the promises of my Father. Remember what God has done for others, He will do it again for you. He makes ways out of no ways just because we are His own.*

Your Children Are Worth the Fight

How long are you willing to fight for your babies, your children's children, and their children? Do not be selfish and think future generations will be ok and will be able to make it through without any help from you. They may not be as strong as you. They may not be able to hold it all together when chaos and trauma are happening all around them, but you can help them out now!

Would you really be ok with your children going through the same things you went through or your father or mother went through? ABSOLUTELY NOT. You should want better for them. Each generation should grow and want more. And when they accomplish more, you should be proud of the fruit of your labor. So, fight for your children…the ones you bore…who share your bloodline and DNA. We have to restore our original bloodline that goes all the way back to our heavenly Father who left us an amazing inheritance to receive.

Generational curses are a very serious subject where people don't realize the depth of the continuous struggles, conclusions, consequences, and regrets that affect our families and future generations. Our choices we make now matter. What we speak matters. Our actions matter now and definitely matter later.

If I had to fight off six generations of junk in my bloodline, it was going to be worth my while, and I was going to win and see victory all across the board. I wasn't going to take no for an answer. I was going to be sure to take back every single thing that had been easily stolen from my bloodline. Note that I said "easily" because we open ourselves up and give the devil legal access to enter our bloodline in one hot second due to our neglect and lack of covering. It's time to have funerals for everything that has been holding on to you for so long. Kill it! Our Savior said, "IT IS FINISHED. The devil has lost.

The enemy will come into parents' minds to make them think they aren't capable of parenting or that they haven't done a good job. That's a lie! It's true that no parent is perfect. We won't always make the right decisions, but we can go out in style trying our very best to raise, develop, and love our children the best we know how. No mother gives birth knowing the entire parenting manual and then memorizing it by heart. We need counsel, godly wisdom and direction. I can't tell you how many times, I have prayed for wisdom regarding certain issues that my children have gone through. As a single parent, I had to have extra eyes to see things about my children. I had to have extra ears and extra knees to pray on as well.

We sometimes miss the mark in certain areas, and some parents have given up and walked away. We see parents sometimes abandoning their parental duties to go in other directions. We see them ignoring their children's needs and overlooking deep inner problems. These things just won't go away if you leave. They have to be brought to the surface. We have to find the root of the issue and get it healed.

It is of the upmost importance for our children to feel their parents' love, support and prayers. If not, ultimately, broken children grow up to be broken adults. Sad kids grow up to be sad adults. Angry kids that have been hurt grow up to be angry adults. Confused kids with parents that are in bisexual, lesbian and gay relationships grow up being confused about themselves. The cycle continues and goes on and on. Adults that were never healed end up doing the same as their parents all over again with their children. I believe this is one major cause for parent/child conflicts and continuous disagreements. Mothers are in conflict with their daughters and fathers are in conflict with their sons. It has to stop and parents must take a stance for change. We have to be their examples. We have to be their strength, their support, and their guidance. We should be life givers and not life takers.

Some children grow up never receiving affection, so they never really know how to love or what love truly is. It's hard to give what you don't have, but we can have love because God is love, and we are made in His image. Love does not hurt. Love gives, and it shows affection even when you may not get it back in return. Love treats others, especially your children more highly than yourself. Love is what God does for us so we are to be the same towards others. He loves us so much.

I wanted the change for my children. I remember apologizing to my two adult children, saying to them in tears that I was sorry they did not have a father in the home and the circumstances surrounding the absence. I apologized because I realized that my daughter doesn't know what an earthly father is like. My son has never experienced an earthly father/son relationship. My grandmother had eight children, and among those eight children, many have different fathers. My mother saw her father once in her whole entire life. It's not natural for children not to know where they came from. Circumstances like this may be common now, but it is definitely not the way things were created to be. Marriages are to be formed and remain and not embittered or end in divorced. Children are to grow up whole and healthy, not broken and angry because of circumstances out of their control.

I have seen children have rebellious spirits and are hurting because of things that their parents may have allowed to happen, seeds that were sown in them, or words spoken over their lives. Rebellion has an originator. Most of the time, there is bitterness and anger because of something that was not received emotional and spiritually. We allow bitterness to enter into our families when we make foolish decisions in our lives that affect their lives later on. When parents put their own lives ahead of their children, it can promote and develop a lifetime of negative effects.

Generations keep inheriting defective DNA's that never get cleansed. Things that go on in the family must be discussed in the home. It's time to throw out all this secrecy stuff. How will anyone get deliverance or even know where to start if nothing is ever spoken about? You can't teach what you don't know and have not learned. You become an adult kid raising another kid that you can't help or assistant with their problems because you are dealing with your own mess from your childhood. You have to get right and make it right with your children.

❖ *"Look, I will send Elijah the prophet to you. He will come before that great and terrible time of judgment from the Lord. Elijah will help the parents become close to their children, and he will help the children become close to their parents…" (Malachi 4:5-6, ERV)*

Continue to pray for the males in your bloodline. Herod was determined to kill all the males because he did not want Jesus to live. This is where brokenness begins in the woman's heart. In Matthew 2:18, Rachel's heart hurt when her seeds were killed. That's why it is so important to build up the male children in our lives so that they won't die spiritually because the weight of the world is on their shoulders. They are leaders and will have their own difficulties to face. They will not have time to be walking around dealing with momma's and granddaddy's problems too.

The devil hunts our men and has previously destroyed generations. We must rebuild our bloodline and make it stronger than ever. How? Fight back and go toe to toe with the enemy. Speak what is not as though it was and watch it come to life. Cover your children with prayer daily, affirm them, and watch the enemy scatter.

Pray for each of your future generations. Sometimes curses skip generations to try to trip you up. You may be thinking everything is good in this area, or I've mastered this area and did not fall into the same trap as my mother or father. But what about your children and grandchildren? Did you fight and war with the enemy, or did you just sit back? You get no results doing nothing. Be smarter and think wiser than the enemy and leave no stone unturned. Because if you stay the course, stay flat footed and don't shake, the weapon won't prosper; instead, it will be destroyed. In scripture, Isaiah set his face like flint, and he knew that he would not be put to shame. (Isaiah 50:7). He was determined, did not move, and depended on God to see him through.

❖ *"Anyone who listens to my teaching and follows it is wise, like a person who builds a house on solid rock. Though the rain comes in torrents and the floodwaters rise and the winds beat against that house, it won't collapse because it is built on bedrock..." (Matthew 7:24-25, NLT)*

Are you ready to fight for your bloodline? Do you want to get rid of that "bad blood" and receive that "new blood" through Christ Jesus? That blood that washes every sin, every blemish, and makes us white as snow? Do you care enough for your family? This challenge should prompt you to want to get down and dirty with the enemy. Get ready, the weapons will form, but they won't prosper. The enemy does not want you to get the wisdom of God's word in order for you to break and unlock the codes. He does not want you walking in freedom and liberty with "clean blood." He wants you, your children, their children, to stay dirty, beat down, depressed, bound, abused, defeated, struggling, and always dealing with some type of problems. Decree that as for me and my household, we will serve the Lord (Joshua 24:15, ESV).

❖ *"For freedom Christ has set us free; stand firm therefore, and do not submit again to a yoke of slavery" (Galatians 5:1, ESV)*

Activate your blood stream that will flow from one generation to another. It belongs to you. Get back what the enemy has stolen from you and your family for years, decades, centuries, and generations. The devil has been robbing you. Are you just going to sit back and let the enemy steal from you freely? We already know what he is here for (to steal, kill and destroy). Parents will do almost anything to protect their children from harm. We would cross an ocean and WE WILL KILL for them, so why would you let him kill your kids, steal their happiness, take their peace, steal their virginity, and inherit generational demons for them to struggle with like you did? You Must Fight For Your Babies!!!

Declaration Prayer

I DECREE that a clean sweep will take place in my family. Wrap me and my children in your arms, Heavenly Father, and never let us go. I bind the strong man of distrust, dishonesty, disloyalty, and dysfunction within my parental guidance. And I pray for restoration, replenishment, reconciliation, and a release for divine turnarounds in our parent/child relationships In the Name of Jesus. These curses will not pass down to my children or any other future generations. They STOP NOW with me in Jesus' Name.

SECTION 4:

CODES UNLOCKED: ACCESS GRANTED

CHAPTER 16

🔓

What's your family legacy? (Generational Inheritances)

❖ *"Beloved, I wish above all things that thou mayest prosper and be in health, even as thy soul prospereth." (3 John 1:2, KJV)*

What inheritance will you leave your family? You were created to develop and cultivate a strong spiritual inheritance within your bloodline. We should be wise and think about the future. The bible declares in Proverbs 13:22 that it is good to have something to pass down to your grandchildren. I'm not only going to leave monetary inheritances to my children and children's children, but it is my prayer, duty, and assignment as a mother of three beautiful creatures that God entrusted me to care for to leave them multitudes of generational blessings. I want them to receive purity and not dirt, peace and not chaos and turmoil, godly mindsets instead of stinking thinking, prosperity and not any type of lack. I will leave them ease and not worry, blessings and not curses. There is no way, they will go through and have the same struggles as my past generations. I've declared, decreed, severed, and broken the chains that tried to hold us back. Understand that our callings and assignments in life are not only for us, but for others. Leviticus 20:22-24 (ESV) says "You shall inherit their land, and I will give it to you to possess, a land flowing with milk and honey, I am the Lord your God, who has separated you from the peoples".

What do you want to inherit? What are you entitled to inherit? Are we not a part of Jesus' bloodline? Are we not sons and daughters of the most high God? Do we not have a Father who sits on the throne who is able to change time, move mountains, shift atmospheres, grow limbs and body parts, give sight to the blind, part the Red Sea, and create the entire universe? Surely, He can cleanse a little blood.

We will build a wealth legacy that will last forever! It's no different than when we set up our earthly legal wills and estate plans. Yes, wealth is an abundance of valuable possessions of money and resources that is well needed; and you may be able to leave your family monetary inheritances, but what about spiritual inheritances because money can't reverse a curse. Money can't help you defeat demons. Money can't help you sleep at night with a peace [shalom] that surpasses all understanding; only the Blood of Jesus can. AMEN! Through His power working in us, we will live the abundant life as promised to us.

❖ *"You shall remember the Lord your God, for it is He who gives you power to get wealth, that He may confirm His covenant that He swore to your fathers, as it is this day." (Deuteronomy 8:18, ESV)*

We have a covenant (a promise, an agreement, a commitment, a guarantee, a pledge, a bond) from God. You have activated the provision in your life so it can be passed down successfully. God has plans for us to prosper in every area of our life. We will succeed!Our children and other family members will succeed as well. We will not rob the next generation of what is rightfully theirs.

❖ *"A good man leaves an inheritance to his children's children, but the sinner's wealth is laid up for the righteous." (Proverbs 13:22, ESV)*

We have more than enough and are living above anything we could think or ask. Thank God for honoring our efforts to make things right. He gives us the opportunity and, in return, He exceeds our expectations. He brings things back and provides us with retroactive pay. He reimburses us and brings restitution and recompense back into our bloodlines. We will receive double for our trouble. We are leaving our families a godly and abundant inheritance in The Name of Jesus!

CHAPTER 17

Moving Forward

Ruth was so desperate for change and something new that she deserted everything she knew and went to an unknown place with people that weren't even her blood family. She stepped out of her comfort zone to cleave to a new life and a new start. The new start was that of much promise and purpose.

After her husband passed away, Ruth decided not to stay in Moab, but to follow Naomi, her mother-in-law, to Bethlehem in Judah. Ruth told Naomi, "For where you go I will go, and where you lodge I will lodge. Your people shall be my people, and your God my God" (Ruth 1:16, ESV). She even went as far as to say, "Where you die I will die, and there I will be buried" (vs. 17). This woman was desperate for change.

Desperation comes from having no one else and nowhere else to turn to. There, in Bethlehem, Ruth met Boaz, who was a man of wealth. He was handsome, had authority, and on top of all that, he provided for Naomi and Ruth. Don't miss out on what God has for you. Keep moving forward even if it is in an unknown territory. I always say "Get comfortable being uncomfortable because it is the only way you will grow." I moved from Georgia to Texas by faith because I was desperate for change. I knew God had more for me in Houston and I trusted and leaned on His guidance and direction to see me through. Within one year, my life had completely changed for the better just like Ruth.

Ruth and Boaz had a son named Obed. Obed was the father of Jesse, who was the father of King David. Through Ruth's new lineage and bloodline with Boaz, our Lord and Savior Jesus Christ was born. She would have never known what would have come out of this choice during such a painful time in her life when her future was unknown.

In the same way, you never know what's up ahead. You won't know until you have faith and make the choice to step out of the norm. Who cares what people say or think. Your life is on the line. The only way you will see change is to make a change in your life. Sometimes big change is required. Sometimes getting away from certain people, blocking numbers, changing numbers, relocating, and switching living situations is the only way out. You know exactly who and what is holding you back. When things haven't worked in the past, the new is the only way to go. Change is inevitable anyway. Change must take place. I dare you to step out on faith and make a move that will benefit you and your future generations. Search for truth as you would search for treasure. Keep going and do not abandon your assignment.

Abraham and Sarah's relationship had dysfunction, but their promised child still came. Even when we bring on the problems ourselves, God can make it work for our good and turn things around. He that began a good work in you will complete it. Even the messiest situations can be our set up. You don't know what is up ahead in your life and in your destiny. You are a new creature created in God's creation. He makes all things new. You have a new bloodline. You have resisted your past and have been redirected by the Lord our God. Take the limits off of God and live in the abundant life that our Savior has prepared for you. He will see you through, He will guide you, but most of all He will deliver you.

You are equipped, you are blessed, and you are free! Follow Him forward and allow Him to be your guide. Mountains in your life cannot withstand the power and the blood of Jesus. Keep going, keep praying, and keep fasting! The mountains will move. Those prayers will be answered, and revelation will be provided. Keep seeking His face, and He will show you the miraculous.

God will sometimes begin preparing you before you even know what He is preparing you for. That's just like our Father to set up us for greatness! Nothing catches Him by surprise. He knew each and every struggle you would have. He knew the loads of past sins that you would have to carry for those unrepentant ancestors of yours. Thank God for His vision for our lives and that He thrusts us into a position that ultimately fulfills our destiny. Let's be drawn to learn more; drawn to experience more; drawn to pray more; drawn to heal and be delivered more. Be drawn to experience that deep connection like never before. Get some accountability. Over time, things will get better and better and easier and easier.

God strengthens our faith to believe deeper and harder. A deeper faith enables Him to move on our behalf. He will perfect our sight to soar above as eagles and equip us for any storm ahead. We will fly above. As you draw closer to Him, he will provide you with keen eye vision and wisdom of strategies to see your way through. He will perfect the things that concern you. You will be upgraded and your thinking will be confident in your God. New dimensions will arise that are full of upgrades and promotions. You will be in alignment with God, and you will finally know your true identity in Christ Jesus.

Where you started is not where you will end. Speak your daily scriptural declarations of breakthrough, future success, new levels of growth, and declare you are an overcomer by faith. Be sure to use affirmations to affirm your faith with positivity and train your mind to think differently about what is seen. Speak those things that you want to see. There is power in what we say. We can speak those strongholds all the way back down to the pits of hell where they belong. DECLARE that your chains are gone. YOU'VE BROKEN THEM. You've gone from death to life and each of your future generations have continued grace that will see them through.

Don't settle for less than what God has for your future. Get rid of the excuses. It's a new day. Know that you will succeed. You will be free, and you WILL BREAK EVERY GENERATIONAL CURSE IN YOUR BLOODLINE.

CHAPTER 18

New Habits, New Cycles, and New BLOOD

Remember, our God is outside of time and goes before us to fix the future. He can straighten any situation out. He can cleanse anything that is dirty. No matter how dark, He can cleanse it whiter than snow. Our times are in His hands and His promises have no expiration dates. He's the one who delivered a 400 year old promise when the walls of Jericho fell down.

Shake off the old mindsets and allow the Father to renew your thinking. As the old saying goes "Out with the old, in with the new." Let the Father upgrade your mind, your thinking, and your circumstances. The old patterns and cycles that have been in your life are being replaced and cleansed with wisdom and direction as you continue on the right path.

Anchor yourself in Him and watch your surrounding situations change for the better. That anchor is what will strengthen you when we surrender our cares to Him. There's no failing in Jesus. His love is unfailing. He's our source of hope, and our only hope. All our hope is in Jesus; and hope is equivalent to trust. We trust in the Lord with all our hearts because we know he has our lives in His hands. You don't need any special ability, just availability. Be open to God's plans and His will for your life.

❖ *"We put our hope in the Lord. He is our help and our shield. In Him, our hearts rejoice, for we trust in His holy name. Let your un-failing love surround us, Lord, for our hope is in you alone". (Psalm 33:20-22, NLT)*

And when we put our trust in Him, we will not be shaken, but our feet will be planted down and we are anchored in Him. We are stabilized and flat footed in Him.

❖ *"And the rain fell, and the floods came, and the winds blew and beat on that house, but it did not fall, because it had been founded on the rock." (Matthew 7:25, ESV)*

If we could actually see what God's intentions are for our lives and the unlimited possibilities we could achieve in Him, it would blow our minds. Take the limits off our King. Know that the plans He has for us are far better and greater than we could ever think or imagine. Let's move forward knowing there is nothing too big for our God. He spoke the entire world into existence. He split the sea in half and killed fear on our behalf. Pastor Joel Osteen always says, "Be a believer and never a doubter".

We are children of God, and He can do anything for anyone. Trust Him. When you begin to move forward, get equipped with the full armor of God. You can't leave home without it. In certain circum-stances, the situations are in your home; so don't go home without the armor. Gird and protect yourself.

❖ *"Therefore, put on every piece of God's armor so you will be able to resist the enemy in the time of evil. Then after the battle you will still be standing firm. Stand your ground, putting on the belt of truth and the body armor of God's righteousness. For shoes, put on the peace that comes from the Good News so that you will be fully prepared. In addition to all of these, hold up the shield of faith to stop the fiery arrows of the devil. Put on salvation as your helmet, and take the sword of the Spirit, which is the word of God." (Ephesians 6:13-17, NLT)*

Please know that when we follow the above scripture and take heed to its instruction of protection, we will indeed be able to stand and have victory, no matter what the enemy or his minions attempt to throw our way. You can do it! You can make the changes necessary to walk and live upright. The change you create will produce a great harvest and become godly cycles and positive habits. Keep passing the tests that come. You are the one who will set the tone for your family. Someone has to start the process, and that someone is you!

Discipline

Be what you desire yourself to be, and discipline will help you to promote the change that is needed in your life. You have to create new cycles and that takes discipline and structure. Discipline is the practice of training yourself to obey rules or a code of behavior in order to correct disobedience. Break away from the old and make up in your mind that you have to keep the good going, no matter how hard it gets. Declare supernatural strength during this process. Fight like your life depends on it (and the lives of others) because it really does.

❖ *"So I do not run aimlessly; I do not box as one beating the air. But I discipline my body and keep it under control, lest after preaching to others I myself should be disqualified." (1 Corinthians 9:26-27, ESV)*

Access Granted

You now have the keys and have unlocked the codes. Let's define what has taken place:

- ♣ The lock was a mechanism used for keeping doors, lids, windows, gates, and so forth fastened in our lives. It provided restricted access to our entryway.

- ♣ Codes required us as users to verify our identity with the right passcode or other forms of authentication.

- ♣ Keys opened the locks for entry...And, we got in!

Congratulations on your new milestone! You have broken barriers, and you have closed doors, but most of all, you have cleansed your bloodline. You are the chosen one! God would not have chosen and sent you to complete this assignment if He thought you weren't capable of handling it with success. The bible says He would put no more on us than we can bear (1 Corinthians 10:13). If God brought it to us, He will definitely bring us through it.

Don't believe the enemy's lies. He may be telling you, you're not spiritual enough, or God could never use you to complete this huge task. Honey, please. You are just the person God wants to use. If He can use Rahab the harlot, and Paul who prosecuted and killed Christians, He can use you too. Honor what God has placed in your care and what He has charged you to do. Make your Daddy proud. Take on extra discipline to achieve this task He has given you authority to take on.

Remember, "To whom much is give, much is required." (Luke 12:48). Remember to take care of what God has blessed you with. Someone once told me that God has given me much responsibility because He knew I could handle it. What an honor it is for God to bless you with a family to care for. It is also a blessing and our responsibility to give great detail and attention to maintaining and protecting our blessings to the best of our abilities. 1 Timothy 5:8 speaks of how everyone should take care of all his or her own people. Most importantly, they should take care of their own family. Genesis 1:28 says for us to be fruitful and multiply. You have activated the blessings in your family, and now you will receive the blessings your ancestors were robbed of.

Declaration Prayer

I decree new life in me as a child of God. I decree that old things have passed away. I am free and a new creature in Christ. I will break every ungodly chain in my life and build a new house, a new temple, a new DNA bloodline. I declare that God's glory is in full operation in my life. I speak wholeness; completeness, and resistance to any demonic cycles. That which God has started in me will be completed. I will accept my God given assignment. I will complete the mission with all power, authority, and with the love. Thank you, Lord, for revelation, knowledge, and wisdom.

I decree and declare that any generational curse, stronghold, hindrance, legality, pattern, or habit is broken and severed in my bloodline. I declare freedom and cleansing from bad blood and speak life to any and all dried-up, dead places with no life. The blood of Jesus is what protected the households in Exodus 12; the enemy will miss me because the blood has already been applied to my life. Breathe new life into me. Repair broken pieces and mend the puzzle of any shattered areas in our lives. Cleanse and refresh my bloodline and circulate pureness unto us, Father. I will produce only the fruit of the spirit daily. I decree a new birth of generations, severed from the shackles of the past, in Jesus' Name. I am rising up with a supernatural anointing, and I'm taking my rightful position as a blood changer. I DECLARE I will live victoriously, for I am a child of the Most High God, and I have his DNA and royal blood flowing through my veins in Jesus' Name AMEN!

My Prayer for you

My prayer is that this book has provided you with solutions and strategies that will carry you through the fight on to victory. I pray that the mind of God will be opened unto you, and the Father will give you power and might to overcome every obstacle as you move forward in your assignment to break generational chains off your life. As you respond to the call, may the God our Father give you revelation, knowledge, and wisdom. Receive it…It's Yours! You've **_Unlocked the Codes_**! In Jesus Name!

References

♣ Caldwell, Suzette (2009). Praying to Change Your Life. (Definition of Prayer)

♣ Clark, Jonas (1998). Jezebel (Witchcraft)

♣ Dictionary.com (2018). https://www.dictionary.com

♣ Dollar, Creflo (2010). Winning in Troubled Times.

♣ Eivaz. Jennifer (2016). Intercessors Handbook (Angels)

♣ Grbich, Natasha (2009). Repentance: Cleansing your generational bloodline

♣ Strong's Concordance. (2018) Expanded Exhaustive Concordance of the Bible

♣ Munroe, Myles (2014). Prayer & Fasting in the kingdom Final Sermon Series. Retrieved from https://youtu.be/LGkAq-2jldY

♣ Graham, Billy (2005). When were the angels created? Retrieved from http://billygraham.org/answer/when-were-the-angels-created-3/

♣ Todd, Mike (2015). Fruits-Fruit Inspection-Root Cause. Retrieved from https://youtu.be/UDCbnBVmp9U

CPSIA information can be obtained
at www.ICGtesting.com
Printed in the USA
LVHW081027241022
731404LV00013B/476

9 781949 826036